Mr. Butler's Statement

Anonymous

The Making of Modern Law collection of legal archives constitutes a genuine revolution in historical legal research because it opens up a wealth of rare and previously inaccessible sources in legal, constitutional, administrative, political, cultural, intellectual, and social history. This unique collection consists of three extensive archives that provide insight into more than 300 years of American and British history. These collections include:

Legal Treatises, 1800-1926: over 20,000 legal treatises provide a comprehensive collection in legal history, business and economics, politics and government.

Trials, 1600-1926: nearly 10,000 titles reveal the drama of famous, infamous, and obscure courtroom cases in America and the British Empire across three centuries.

Primary Sources, 1620-1926: includes reports, statutes and regulations in American history, including early state codes, municipal ordinances, constitutional conventions and compilations, and law dictionaries.

These archives provide a unique research tool for tracking the development of our modern legal system and how it has affected our culture, government, business – nearly every aspect of our everyday life. For the first time, these high-quality digital scans of original works are available via print-on-demand, making them readily accessible to libraries, students, independent scholars, and readers of all ages.

The BiblioLife Network

This project was made possible in part by the BiblioLife Network (BLN), a project aimed at addressing some of the huge challenges facing book preservationists around the world. The BLN includes libraries, library networks, archives, subject matter experts, online communities and library service providers. We believe every book ever published should be available as a high-quality print reproduction; printed on-demand anywhere in the world. This insures the ongoing accessibility of the content and helps generate sustainable revenue for the libraries and organizations that work to preserve these important materials.

The following book is in the "public domain" and represents an authentic reproduction of the text as printed by the original publisher. While we have attempted to accurately maintain the integrity of the original work, there are sometimes problems with the original work or the micro-film from which the books were digitized. This can result in minor errors in reproduction. Possible imperfections include missing and blurred pages, poor pictures, markings and other reproduction issues beyond our control. Because this work is culturally important, we have made it available as part of our commitment to protecting, preserving, and promoting the world's literature.

GUIDE TO FOLD-OUTS MAPS and OVERSIZED IMAGES

The book you are reading was digitized from microfilm captured over the past thirty to forty years. Years after the creation of the original microfilm, the book was converted to digital files and made available in an online database.

In an online database, page images do not need to conform to the size restrictions found in a printed book. When converting these images back into a printed bound book, the page sizes are standardized in ways that maintain the detail of the original. For large images, such as fold-out maps, the original page image is split into two or more pages

Guidelines used to determine how to split the page image follows:

• Some images are split vertically; large images require vertical and horizontal splits.
• For horizontal splits, the content is split left to right.
• For vertical splits, the content is split from top to bottom.
• For both vertical and horizontal splits, the image is processed from top left to bottom right.

MR. BUTLER'S

STATEMENT,

ORIGINALLY PREPARED

IN AID OF HIS

PROFESSIONAL COUNSEL

BUTLER vs BUTLER.

Extract from the Opinion of the Court of Common Pleas, delivered by the Hon Edward King, President Judge, January 20th, 1849

PIERCE BUTLER LIBELLANT,

FRANCIS ANNE BUTLER RESPONDENT

vs

" The libellant in this libel which is in the brief and sententious form peculiar to our practice, sets forth that his wife, the respondent, did, in violation of her matrimonial obligations, on the 11th of September, 1845, wilfully, maliciously, and without reasonable cause, desert and absent herself from him and his habitation, and since that time has continuously persisted in such desertion and absence It concludes with a prayer for the divorce from the bond of matrimony, given by the Act of Assembly to the injured party under such circumstances To this libel the respondent, Francis Anne Butler, has answered in which answer, she first denies that on the 11th day of September, 1845, or at any other time before or since, she had wilfully and maliciously deserted and absented herself from the libellant and his habitation She then proceeds to state, that it was true, and that she therefore admits, that she did leave and absent herself from the habitation of the libellant on the 10th day of September, 1845, and that she has ever since remained so absent But she denies such leaving and absence to have been desertion First.

Because for a long time previous the libellant had separated himself from her as a husband, and because of his wrongful and unlawful conduct towards her while in his habitation, which would have justified her in quitting it, without incurring the legal consequences of desertion Second Because she had the assent and license of the libellant so to quit his habitation, and absent herself from it, and his subsequent approval and acquiescence therein, and also, because his conduct to her for a long space of time before she so quitted and absented herself was designed and calculated and such as to force her therefrom Third Because she would have been justified in so absenting herself without such license, approval, acquiescence, or design, by the libellant's cruel treatment of her and by such personal indignities offered by him to her as rendered her condition intolerable and life burdensome She then 'craves leave to submit' what she terms a 'Narrative in support of these allegations, which 'Narrative,' with its subjoined exhibits, occupies nearly sixty printed pages At the conclusion of this Narrative, she asks that her cause may be tried by a jury, on an issue or issues, to be framed for that purpose— a right given to her by Act of Assembly

"Independent of this historical sketch of matrimonial discords, the answer, like the libel would have been in perfect concord with our simple, facile and convenient practice in the administration of the divorce laws. It would have been the brief, but clear and precise, assignment of causes, why the respondent had quitted and absented herself from the common habitation, and the negation that such quitting and absence was a wilful and malicious abandonment of her marriage duties The parties would thus have reached a complete issue, and the cause, according to our practice, have been ripe for a hearing, either before the Court, if a jury trial had not been asked, or before a jury, if such a claim had been interposed

"Previous, however, to proceeding to trial, the libellant would have had the right to demand and receive of the respondent, a written specification of the acts of cruelty, or other circumstances, by which she proposed supporting her general allegations, with the times, places, and circumstances of their occurrence as far as these could be reasonably and practicably given. The giving of such notice would not have made the facts contained in it, evidence of course in the cause. On the trial all such matters as should have been deemed inadmissible on the ground of irrelevancy or inadequacy, could have been objected to when offered, and would have been admitted or rejected by the judge who presided at the trial according as he considered the objections taken valid or otherwise.

"Why this course was not pursued—this regular, usual and orderly course—arises from the useless introduction of Mrs. Butler's 'Narrative' into the answer which the libellant seeks to treat as if it were a responsive allegation, in an English Ecclesiastical Court.

. . . .

'In her denial of the wilful and malicious desertion charged against her in the libel—in assigning the libellant's license and cruelty as justificatory reasons for her departure from the common habitation, the respondent did all she was required to do, in order to demand that this fact should be tried by jury. If specially called upon before such trial, to precise statements of the facts intended to be relied upon by her to sustain her answer, and which the libellant may regard as too generally charged therein, she is bound to furnish them. All the matter, however, introduced into the answer in the shape of a 'Narrative' is pure surplusage—a statement of facts, some of which would, and some of which would not be received in evidence on the trial. It is therefore not the subject of exception, either as to its form or substance. Being extraneous to the formal record, it must be stricken from it. The exceptions of course fall with it. The case is thus brought back to its true and simple elements, and made to assimilate its features to the hundreds of other analogous causes which occupy the Courts of the Commonwealth. The libel will then charge against the respondent a wilful and malicious desertion, without reasonable cause, of her husband and his habitation, persisted in for two years The answer will deny such wilful and malicious desertion, and assert that an admitted quitting of and absence from the common habitation, by the respondent, was licensed by the express assent of the libellant, or justified by law from *reasonable* causes supervening, viz unkind treatment and cruelty on the part of the husband The issue between the parties under our practice will be thus completely formed, and ripe for trial by jury On the trial the jury must decide whether such abandonment of the common domicil was with the previous license and assent, or subsequent approbation and approval of the husband, or, if the respondent fails in establishing this position, whether the unkind treatment and cruelty of the husband towards her was of that character which formed a reasonable cause for her departure

" In thus determining that the cause has been submitted to us, in a manner which does not regularly raise the questions of fact so elaborately discussed we are not to be understood as in the slightest degree expressing any opinion on the merits of the controversy When the case has been submitted to a jury—when the facts on both sides have been fully heard—the time will have arrived for such an expression of opinion *Before* such expression would be certainly premature and might be grossly unjust Indeed, it scarcely could be otherwise than unjust, because it would be formed on a one-sided view of the subject "

Most persons on reading the concluding paragraph of the foregoing extract from the opinion of the Court, will learn perhaps for the first time, that but one side of this controversy has ever publicly appeared, namely that embodied in the *Narrative*" of the respondent The argument before the Court was merely on the position taken by the libellant's counsel that the answer of the respondent, even conceding its denied statements showed no sufficient cause to delay the judgment of the Court, or to warrant a trial by jury The Court decided that the *Narrative* of the answer was irregularly introduced that it should be struck or withdrawn from the record that the case should upon the short and usual pleadings, be submitted to a jury agreeably to the Act of Assembly, and the foregoing extract is taken from the opinion delivered on that occasion This opinion was pronounced January 20 1849, and the issues were set down for trial on April 16 The following exposition, or brief, was prepared by me for the instruction of the gentlemen who were to conduct my cause, and was put into their hands more than a year ago The trial was subsequently postponed on motion of counsel for the respondent from April until September, 1849 It was, however never tried nor further argued, judgment having been entered by default against the respondent, whose appearance to the suit was retracted before the time for trial arrived

Having succeeded in obtaining the prayer of my petition—a decree of divorce from the bond of matrimony—I would willingly allow the matter to rest, but the opinion of those friends on whose judgment I most rely is so opposed to such a course, that I am induced to print this review of facts My friends require it of me It is not intended as a publication and I have taken every possible precautionary step against its being so perverted by others My object is not to assail or to depreciate, it is merely self-vindication, a right belonging to every one, and a duty which we owe not less to ourselves, than to our friends, our kindred, and our children

As this Statement was originally intended for the

use of my counsel and as I relied mainly upon it to secure a successful issue of my suit, I have inserted nothing not susceptible of legal proof. In printing it some portions are forborne, as they were not necessary to my own vindication.

Philadelphia, March, 1850

MORAL TRAITS

One reason and perhaps the fundamental one, for the ill success which attended my marriage will readily be found in the peculiar views which were entertained by Mrs Butler on the subject of marriage and her unwillingness to abide by the express and inculcated obligations of that contract. She held that marriage should be companionship on equal terms—partnership, in which if both partners agree, it is well but if they do not, neither is bound to yield—and that at no time has one partner a right to control the other. Some of her views on this subject will be found in the subjoined extracts from her own letters.

> 11 *Park Place, St James's,*
> " *Tuesday June 20th.*"
> [London, 1857]

* * * 'My dearest husband: You ask me if this separation has not strengthened our affection and our value for each

---

* The separation alluded to was this —In the year 1836 two years and a half after my marriage it became necessary that I should go to the State of Georgia, on a visit to my property there. My absence was to continue for several months and Mrs Butler expressing a desire to spend that period in her native country, I cheerfully acceded to her wishes and she sailed from New York in the packet ship South America, on November 1 1836 taking with her our only child then a year and a half old, and its nurse. They

B

other? If it has endeared me to you I ought to be grateful to it, and I think that it has led me to reflect upon some passages of our intercourse with self-condemnation, and a desire to discharge my duty to you more faithfully, than I may hitherto have done. Yet do not now mistake me—you ask me in your last, how I like my independence, and whether I remember how vehemently and frequently I objected to your control over my actions. I remember this well and part of my regret in contemplating the past arises from the *manner* of my resistance, not the fact itself. Whether one person can or ought to exercise control over another, I think is a question your own justice and good sense would answer at once. Neither my absence from you, nor my earnest desire to be again with you can make me admit that the blessed and happy relationship, in which we stand to each other, is any thing but perfect companionship, perfect friendship, perfect love. For the existence of these, justice must also exist, and there is no justice in the theory, that one rational creature is to be subservient to another, nor can there be any high or holy feeling where there is not freedom and independence. Why, the great God who made us has not trammelled our free will, and shall we claim of each other that which the Omnipotent has refrained from demanding? But, dear Pierce, upon what ground should you exercise this control over me? Is it because having full power to withhold the gift I freely gave myself to you, to add as much by my fellowship as I could to your happiness? Is it because you are better than myself? I am sure you will not say so, whatever I may think. Is it because you are more enlightened, more intellectual? You know that is not so, for your opportunities have not been the same. Is it because you are stronger in body? Now I know that

arrived in England on the 27th of the same month, and immediately went to her father's house in London whence the above letter was written. At its date we had been separated nearly eight months. I crossed the Atlantic and joined her in August, 1837, and after a very short stay there, returned to this country in October following, bringing Mrs Butler and our child with me

I might as well spare writing all this, for your mind is much the same as my own upon this matter, as your whole conduct to me has proved. If, indeed, you do not admit and respect the rights of your wife, how comes it that she is at this moment an independent agent, having been so for upwards of six months, with the precious charge of your darling child, and the free and generous use of your means. I am sure, dearest Pierce, I ought to be little anxious to argue the point, possessed as I am of every real advantage which your admission of it could bestow on me, but for this, that I would rather hear you acknowledge a principle of truth, than enjoy the utmost indulgence that your affection could bestow upon me." * * * *

The next extract, and the letter which follows it were written in London, at the time of our second and more prolonged visit to England.

[London 1842.]

* * *   I will now say something upon the subject of the obedience which you claim from me. It does not enter into the marriage contract as performed in the Church[†] to which I belong, and of which if you belong to any, you are also a member. It is not in the law of my conscience to promise implicit obedience to a human being, fallible like myself, and who can by no means relieve me of the responsibility of my actions before God. Upon these grounds I could not promise obedience to any one." * * *

---

* In this, and in all other letters adduced, asterisks (* * *) will be found wherever there are omissions; where no asterisks appear, the letters are inserted entire.

† This remark has reference to the Unitarian Church, to which Mrs Butler became a convert after our marriage; for she was educated in the tenets of the Church of England, was a communicant in that church, and the ceremony by which we were united was that of the ritual of the Episcopal Church, performed in Christ Church, Philadelphia, by the Right Reverend Bishop White.

"I have already promised to *endeavour* to control my temper—to promise more, with my nervous, excitable temperament, and the temptations to irritation which naturally spring out of our differences of disposition would be unwise and unwarrantable. My temper—or, as I must be allowed to call it, my temperament—will probably furnish me with severe moral labour, and those who love me and live with me with exercise for their forbearance and charity until I die. I cannot therefore *promise* to govern it, for that will probably be my life's lesson, in which my friends I trust will help, not hinder me. For your second condition that I will *submit myself to your will* I am sorry to say that I cannot entertain this proposal for a moment. I consider it my duty *not* to submit my conduct to the government of any other human being, but could I for a moment think of giving my conscience into other hands than my own—*which is precisely the same thing*—though I love you better than any other living creature, my affection does not so far blind my judgment as to suggest you as fit for such a charge; and indeed the few persons I know who appear to me to be so, would conscientiously shrink from such an undue responsibility. I am sorry you wrote me what you did, though when I had read but the first line, I was on the point of running to your room; for your first condition I had already promised to conform to with my most earnest endeavour, and your second I had already told you most distinctly I never *could* accede to."

I think these letters sufficiently prove that Mrs Butler's opinions, with regard to the duties of a wife towards her husband, were peculiar and impracticable.

Another source of our difficulties will be found in the structure of Mrs Butler's mind. There are two strongly marked features in her character—great en-

ergy of will and a decided preference for her own
judgment and opinions over those of every other person. Hence arose that sense of imagined oppression
of which she so constantly complained, and which led
her to offer a perverse opposition not only on points
of importance, but on matters comparatively insignifi-
cant and to exhibit nonconformity and an unyielding
spirit in every thing.

One painful subject of difference between us, was
that of negro slavery. Although we resided in Penn-
sylvania where slavery does not exist, the greater
part of my property lies in the State of Georgia, and
consists of plantations and negroes. Mrs. Butler,
after our marriage, not before, declared herself to be
in principle an abolitionist, and her opinions were
frequently expressed in a violent and offensive manner. this was grievous enough to bear, however, I
seldom opposed or combatted them, but when it
came to the point of publishing her sentiments, I offered the most unqualified opposition to it.

An event of this nature occurred in 1840. We
were living at the time at our home about six miles
from Philadelphia. She was solicited by letter from
an entire stranger, to contribute a composition to a
small work to be printed, and to be sold at an anti-
slavery fair about to be held in Philadelphia. I was
greatly provoked at the application, but my feeling
was changed to the deepest pain and mortification,
when I found that my wife intended to comply with
the request. I entreated her not to do so. I represented to her the shameless indelicacy on the part of
the abolitionists in attempting to enlist the wife of a

slave owner—that her aiding them by a contribution from her pen would be arraying herself on their side, and against the character, position, and interests of her husband, and that their triumph would be my humiliation I told her that it would be impossible for her ever again to accompany me when I went to visit my estate in the south, and that it might even be unsafe for myself to do so, unless I showed, by some decided measure, that I did not coincide with her in opinion, which it might embarrass me to do satisfactorily since very few could believe that it was out of a husband's power to control his wife, in a matter of such vital importance to their common interests But all was vain, she heeded me not, neither entreaties nor arguments moved her she sent the contribution, and it was published with her name This was the deepest wound my spirit had as yet received at her hands

Not long after this event she referred to it in a letter she wrote me from the city where she was passing two or three days

"*Monday, November* 23 " [1840]

*   *   *   *   "The event which occurred lately, and led to so much bitterness between us, caused you deep pain, but oh think how I was tried, who, to fulfil what I conceived was right, had to disregard your dear entreaties, and to bear up as I might, under the utter bereavement and desolation of your alienated affection The sacred plea I used seemed light to you, while I daily and hourly sacrifice to your perception of right, in my mode of living and the means by which I subsist, all that I think vital in existence—justice, mercy, and self-respect "   *   *   *

"The sacred plea' she used was, that she considered it her duty to assist the anti-slavery cause whenever she had it in her power to do so and the "sacrifice of all that she thought vital in existence" consisted in her consenting as my wife to be supported out of means derived from the labour of slaves

An occurrence of a similar nature took place during my second visit to England, when I was residing with my family in London A lady editing an anti-slavery paper in New York wrote to Mrs Butler, and asked, as a contribution, for some portions of a journal which it was understood she had kept while in Georgia Again I used entreaty and remonstrance to induce her to disregard this request, or to refuse it, but as on the former occasion, it was to no purpose This lady was a stranger to her, except by name yet she immediately assented to her wishes, and wrote her the following letter —

> "81 *Harley Street,*
> ' *Tuesday, November 2d* "
> [London 1841]

"My dear Madam.

"That part of my southern journal which was written on my husband's slave estates, would be, I suppose, at once the most interesting and the most useful to the publication for which you request me to furnish you matter, but I do not feel at liberty to give that to the public or I should have done so long ago It is possible however, that what I wrote on my way to Mr Butler's plantation, may be of use or interest to you, and that I should be very happy to place at your disposal This would consist of about four or five longish letters, containing the account of my journey from Philadelphia to Georgia, in the course of which, some observations on the effects of slavery as they were apparent wherever I went, necessarily occur. I am sorry that it is not in my power to do more than this, and only hope that what I offer may prove of the least use to you. Pray let me know, if you accept this, how I shall get it conveyed to you.

"I am, my dear Madam

' Yours very truly,

' FANNY BUTLER "

This letter together with several others was given to me by Mrs Butler, for the purpose of being sealed and forwarded as was her custom. I intentionally omitted sending it, and threw it into a drawer of my writing table, where it was found by her after a lapse of some weeks. When she understood that I had purposely kept it back, she evinced great anger, and immediately wrote another letter to the lady highly offensive and contemptuous towards myself, wherein she entered into all the details of the occurrence, and told her the reason of her not having received an answer to her application. I warned her, that if she sent a letter so derogatory to me, it might lead to our separation; that it would probably be published, and if so, it would be impossible for us to live together any longer. Still that letter was sent. I now felt myself most painfully circumstanced, on its way to the editress of an anti-slavery newspaper, I feared it would soon grace the columns of that journal, and so inevitably sunder us forever. I scarcely knew what to do, but resolved on an effort to prevent the catastrophe. I accordingly wrote to a lady in this country, a friend of Mrs Butler's, and an acquaintance,

as I believed of the editress. This lady also entertained decided anti-slavery sentiments. I detailed the
circumstances, and asked her to request the editress
not to publish Mrs Butler's communication, or at
least not to do so without an express sanction from
Mrs Butler. I begged her to write to Mrs Butler
on the subject; she complied with both requests,
wrote to Mrs Butler strongly urging her not to allow the letter to be printed and advising her against
contributing to the paper. This exhortation, coming
from a friend, who like herself was an abolitionist,
produced a compliance: with what grace she complied will be seen by the letter she wrote to the editress on the occasion.

"*Harley Street*

Friday, April 1st"

[London, 1842.]

' Madam,

'I must request that you will have the kindness not to publish
the letter which I wrote you a short time ago; and at the same time
must inform you, that I intend to break my promise with regard to
the papers which I promised to furnish you for publication, upon the
subject of my southern journey. I can add nothing to this but the
assurance, that however great your contempt may be for my want
of purpose, or your indignation for this proceeding it cannot possibly exceed my own.

"I am, Madam

'Yours truly

"FANNY BUTLER'

The following note to myself, was written a short
time subsequent to the date of the above.

＊　　　＊　　　＊　　　＊　 "You have often asserted that I *never*
in *any single* instance have conformed to your will or complied

C

with your wishes I must now bring to your recollection, that
within the last six months I have *twice* yielded to your will in matters of considerable importance once, I am ashamed to say, in a
matter of conscience and once in one which concerned my own gratification very deeply In the first instance I resisted your desire
very long and very earnestly, because it was a point of conscience
which I never ought to have given up nevertheless I finally did so,
though labouring under my own condemnation, both at the time and
ever since, on that account The other point, the publishing of my
tragedy, I gave up also, and I must beg to remind you, without a
single remonstrance or attempt at resistance, *because* it was a thing
that concerned my own gratification solely Having made this protest against your statement which, with such exceptions as these
can hardly be considered a just one, I will say no more but this"——

The 'point of conscience' which Mrs Butler condemns herself for having yielded, was the sending her
southern journal to be published in an anti-slavery
paper, but she forgets that it was not yielded to my
request, but at the remonstrance of her friend in
America to whom I had written so that the justice
which I sought at her hands was not granted to me,
but to a third person, who had certainly far less claim
to her consideration than myself

Mrs. Butler s opinions and views in regard to the
marriage contract and negro slavery, were either not
formed or not expressed before she became my wife,
a knowledge of them or either of them, as they were
afterwards exhibited, must have proved an insupera-
ble bar to our union

Mrs Butler also forgets that the second point she

cites—the publication of her tragedy—was not conceded to any solicitation of mine. The story of this tragedy was of a nature to cause me both pain and regret that she had selected it for an exercise of her talents. When it was written—1838—I objected to its publication; but she was so bent on its seeing the light in some way, that I consented to its being sent to London and offered for representation there. She accordingly addressed Mr. Macready—at that time lessee of Covent Garden theatre—and sent him her play for representation on the stage. Mr. Macready wrote her two very courteous replies on the subject, with the second returning the manuscript. He spoke in admiration of the production as ' full of truth, of ' power and exquisite beauty ' and he added ' but ' the plot is of such a startling character that I have 'been for several days in a state of perplexity how "to proceed. I have at last resolved upon a course, ' which I trust you will approve. I have delivered the manuscript to Mr. Harness expressing to him ' my high opinion of the genius that sustains it ' throughout at such an even height, and adding that ' its merit *challenges* representation,—but that the ' danger of its plot induces me from sentiments of "the highest admiration and respect for the author, to place it in his hands in order that he may ascer-"tain for me the opinion of her friends as to whe-"ther the probable experiment of this play upon the "stage would be gratifying in its result to herself and "them. I hope I shall have met your wishes in what "I have done. Whatever be the opinion returned to " me by Mr. Harness, I feel quite certain that as the "author of such a work, you should not quarrel with

' its suppression proving, as you do a power within
you to establish such a reputation in dramatic lite-
' rature as none of your sex have ever yet approach-
' ed   The letter from which I quote is dated   Co-
' vent Garden Theatre London January 5, 1839 '

I have not been able to find Mr Macready's second
letter but he apprized her that the decision of Mr
Harness and her other friends was against the representation of her tragedy, and, accordingly, he returned it

I considered this decision coming from her own
country and her special friends as for ever precluding
the publication for the reason— the startling character of the plot '—which caused its suppression'
from the stage was of equal weight to prevent its
being put in print

Nor did Mrs Butler again agitate the matter for
more than three years after this adverse judgment
When she did so and proposed to publish the play I
of course discountenanced it

Her ' protest ' is therefore unfortunate   As the
' twice in six months ' which she adduces for evidence that she sometimes yielded to my will ' were
in fact submissions to the advice of others, after she
had repelled mine

Another topic, which not unfrequently embittered
our fireside intercourse was a spirit of unwise com-
parison constantly indulged between my country and
her own   She came to the United States with a prejudice amounting to hatred *   Almost every thing

---

* She has herself recorded the ' hatred' —her own word—she felt towards
America, before she ever saw the country or knew its people

which she found different from what she was accustomed to, was pronounced to be inferior and wrong As I never visited England until some years after my marriage I was unable to controvert many of her unfavourable comparisons, which now since I have resided in England I know to be unjust and unfounded Oftentimes when she would express opinions and pronounce judgment in her accustomed tone of infallibility disadvantageous to America I could only sit by and listen in mortified silence, for then I knew only my own country

Having thus directed attention to some of Mrs Butler's mental peculiarities I will now show the results and consequences of her acting upon them I begin at the date of my marriage and proceed regularly in the order of time from that epoch

AT HOME

My marriage took place on June 7th, 1834 and it was Mrs Butler's choice as well as my own, to reside in the country The place selected for our residence was a family country seat about six miles from Philadelphia We did not however go to it at once, we passed the summer in travelling, and at a watering place, and in the autumn we stayed for three months at my brothers house in Philadelphia During this period, Mrs Butler was engaged in preparing her "Journal" for the press I was much averse to the publication of that work it was the private diary of a young woman, and contained much that was unfit for the public eye, but it was sold to the publishers previous to our marriage and they would not relinquish their contract I found it necessary for her own sake that many things should be omitted, and accordingly I read the manuscript and proof sheets Any curtailment greatly irritated her she opposed the slightest alteration after it was copied for the printer, and as she objected so vehemently to it I struck out as little as possible, and indeed passed over many parts that I would certainly otherwise have erased Every sentence, and even word, that I wished to omit or

after was stoutly defended and my suggestions made
her very angry At length she declared she would
not submit to further curtailment in her composition
but would leave me This occurred in November
1831, less than six months after our marriage, while
we were residing temporarily with my brother She
packed up her clothes and other things, which occupied her two days about 6 o'clock in the evening of
the second day, after it was dark and when I happened to be out of the way, she left the house alone I
went into her room shortly afterward, discovered that
she was gone and found the following note on her
table This farewell is somewhat girlish and roman-
tic but she had rather passed the age of girlhood at
this time, having completed her twenty-fifth year

"I believe I do not owe a cent in the City, if, however, there
should be any claims which I have forgotten, the enclosed twenty
dollars must answer them fully, therefore any demands that may be
made upon you in my name are unjust. If I send a porter for my
things perhaps you will be so good as to let him have them and if
you will be at the further trouble of sending my poor little bird
down to Rose Sully, you will much oblige,

"FANNY"

I could do nothing, for I knew not where to go in
search of her Between nine and ten o'clock, however, she came back, went into her room, threw herself on the bed, and lay there all night without un-
dressing She did not speak to me nor I to her I
had suffered great anxiety while she was out of the
house, and I was at once so much pained by her wil-
fulness and so much relieved by her return, as to be

well content to allow her to remain undisturbed She
slept, the next morning she seemed to be in a better
state of feeling, I then spoke to her and anger having subsided, I prevailed on her to be friends with
me again   At first she would not tell me where she
had gone, but after a day or two she stated that having resolved to return to England, she left the house
to seek a public hotel she wished to find one that
she remembered to have passed somewhere in North
Second or Third street which was far from our residence and where as she thought, it would not occur
to me to look for her at the time she was not well
acquainted with the streets of Philadelphia and after
walking for about three hours without finding the
hotel, she returned for the night, intending however,
to start off again the next morning

On the first day of January 1835, we went to our
country seat, where, in May of that year, our first
child was born   During the period that Mrs Butler
was in expectation of becoming a mother she manifested habitual discontent, frequently expressing regret at having married me, and a desire for release
from an union which appeared already to have become distasteful and irksome to her, and she was
constantly wishing to return to her native country I
looked upon these expressions as merely perverse fancies, to be dispelled by the birth of her child, and I
sometimes assured her that if she continued in the
same mind after that event, I would not oppose her
wishes, supposing that I should hear no more about
it   It did not however turn out as I had expected,
for after her child was born she was as strongly bent

upon going away as before   The following letter in which she evinces a desire to abandon her infant was written in 1835, about three months after its birth

*   *   *   * " I must claim the fulfilment of a promise you often reiterated to me during my pregnancy, that I should be allowed to return to England, after the birth of my child   I am weary of my useless existence, my superintendence in your house is nominal, you have never allowed it to be otherwise, you will suffer no inconvenience from its cessation   *   *   *
Under these circumstances I must again beg that you will perform your promise of sending me to England, when my child was born If you procure a healthy nurse for the baby she will not suffer, and, provided she is fed, she will not fret after me   Had I died when she was born you must have taken this measure, and my parting from her now will be to her as though she had never known me, and to me far less miserable than at any future time   I must beg you will take measures for my going away , and have only to regret that I am not other than I am, perhaps I might have been happier myself, and possessed qualities more acceptable to you than those with which nature and education have endowed me.

" FANNY

It is scarcely necessary to say that I did not ' take measures for her going away," but rather sought by kindness and by every means in my power to promote a feeling of greater contentment

We remained at home for nearly two years , namely, until the end of October, 1836 at that time, as I have explained in a note at page 9, Mrs Butler went to visit her family and friends in England , she was absent nearly twelve months, and returned in Octo-

D

ber, 1837 I had gone to England and joined her a short time before her return We once again—in December, 1837—went to reside in the country

From that period her morbid discontent became so great and was so continually expressed, that a mere narration of it, and of its effects, would scarcely be credited indeed, but for the existence of some of her own letters, written at the time, and constantly referring to her state of mind, I should be unable to convey any idea of it without risking my own credibility I will therefore insert her letters, contenting myself with remarking that no causes whatever existed for the state of feeling they delineate except such as were self-created and imaginary

The following letter was written in the early part of 1838, when she was in expectation of becoming a mother for the second time

· You will oblige me by taking immediate means for my return to my own family Since my marriage with you my life has been one of incessant privation, which was all very well while you were kind to me, as however I will never be subject to rudeness and ill manners from any one, without doing that which is in my power to avoid it I must now beg that you will take proper means for my leaving you, as you were the only thing that kept me in this country I will not return to the farm any more, but till you can make arrangements for my going to England I will either remain here, at the corner of Chestnut and Eighth streets, or go to an inn, whichever you like best. If you do not choose to take these steps, I have my watch and gold chain with me, which will get me sufficient money to go home in some manner or other, and I will make that use of them forthwith Be so good as to leave some answer here when you go out of town, and I shall come for it There is abundance of time for me to reach England before my confinement, and if you will hereafter appoint means for your child's being brought over to you. I shall, of course, observe them. With regard to myself, I need not trouble you further than just to ask you for as much money as will take me to London, which, however, if you should feel disinclined to do, I will find some means of accomplishing myself."

I deny the justness of the charge of "rudeness," which is brought against me in the preceding letter. It may well be believed that a man's disposition, and consequently, his manners, would not be entirely unruffled when his spirits were so depressed and harrassed as mine were by such conduct, and, if Mrs Butler's incessant fault-finding and dissatisfaction with every thing around her, made me, at times, irritable, I can only say, it would not have been so if she had rendered my fireside cheerful and peaceful, but I do not think I can justly be charged with any sort of rudeness towards her at any time.

The following letter was written in the autumn of the same year, 1838, after the birth of our second child.

" You are now again relieved from my presence,* and if you will take my advice and casting aside your regard for appearances consult only your own comfort and happiness you will make some arrangements by which in future to be freed from it altogether. My feelings towards you, and with regard to my own situation, are such as to render it utterly impossible for me calmly to speak upon the subject, but I yet think it necessary that you should understand in some measure what they are,—as perhaps your own sense of justice may induce you then not entirely to disregard them. I believe you do

* This refers to my being temporarily in Philadelphia.

not yourself think the state in which we live when on good terms
with each other, one of very intimate companionship or confidence;
nature has most blessedly, for you, rendered the sympathy and communion of others totally unnecessary to you, and, were it otherwise, you are here in the midst of your own people and kindred, and
in your own country and all the sources from whence such intercourse could flow are open around you if you pleased to draw from
them. That the case is the very reverse with me, I need not trouble you to read, and that I am by nature as dependent upon sympathy and mental companionship, as by circumstances deprived of any
and all such, you are as well aware as I am In part this is my own
fault. for I married you without, for a moment, using my judgment
or observation to ascertain whether or not we were likely to be companions and fellows to each other I, above all women, was bound
not to neglect this consideration, since, in marrying in a strange
country, I at once broke the thread and for ever, of all former inti-
macies, friendships and affections Our intercourse, then, was never fellowship, most certainly the time is now evidently come
when the sentiment which drew us together is waning and perishing
away · this is natural,—it was of an order which can never long
survive intimacy and possession, and they who have no other bond
of union must, after a very brief space, cease to have any. There
is, however, one tie by which I am bound to you,—that of utter dependence upon your means, and, therefore, of necessity, upon your
will. Such a bond as this, though borne by many women, must
needs be irksome to one who has the least feeling or pride how
doubly irksome then to me, who have had and still have the means
of perfect independence in my own power, in the exercise of a
distasteful profession, it is true, but, at all events, unfettered by the
very odious restraint of obligation without affection. This feeling
of my present position often and most painfully draws my wishes
back to my own country and friends, and my heart, which certainly
has found no home here, for ever yearns most painfully after those

early ties which it renounced for a residence in a strange country, among strangers   ⁎   ⁎   ⁎   ⁎   Could food and raiment content me, and the possession of the physical comforts of life, doubtless I have every reason to be contented or could the society of two infants and my servants atone to me for that which I habitually enjoyed in my own country, I might not complain of the mental solitude in which I live. If hitherto, however, my want of cheerfulness has dissausfied you, I fear it may do so yet more henceforth, for, since my last confinement, I have been suffering incessantly from painful and exhausting indisposition, and I fear that the loss of my health will not tend much to improve my spirits upon this ground, therefore, I think your comfort will probably be increased by your absence from me   ⁎   ⁎   ⁎   ⁎   ⁎

"These considerations, and the conviction that though my companionship is no source of pleasure to you, my conduct is frequently one of annoyance, induce me to propose that we may henceforward live apart, my discontents will then no longer vex you, nor the restraints to which I am now subject, gall and irritate me."   ⁎   ⁎

In the same year, 1838, I went, for the second time, to visit my property, and to attend to my affairs, in Georgia, and I was accompanied by Mrs Butler and my two children, it was her first and only visit to the south We passed the winter on my plantations, and for a time the entire change of scene and manner of life had the effect of dispelling some of her discontent, but it was only for a time, for the winter did not pass without much trouble between us, and a full share of the domestic unhappiness which her conduct brought upon me More than once she renewed her desire to leave her family and to return to England, and on one occasion she was apparently so fixed in this resolve, that for a time I gave up all hope of being able to dissuade her from it   On this occasion she actually left her children for three days and probably would have done so entirely had there been any means of her getting away, but, fortunately, no steamboat left Darien—the nearest town—during this time, and before there was an opportunity to get away I succeeded in inducing her to return to her children   As this circumstance is referred to in another place,* I need not say more about it here

We returned to the north in April, 1839, and again went to our home in the vicinity of Philadelphia

The state of her mind and feelings at that period will be exhibited by letters she then wrote which render unnecessary any comment or explanation on my part

The following was addressed to me not long after our return from Georgia

*   *   *   *   " It might seem indelicate to urge upon you the sacrifices I have made, and the trials I have embraced, in marrying you, yet, as disappointment in the looked-for compensation, which would have made the sacrifice easy and the trials light, now often turns my thoughts upon this subject, I must speak of the change in my situation, as I feel it.   I have left my country with many women this would mean little or nothing, but I have national attachments so strong as to amount to prejudices, and the customs, habits, and even the lovely outward face of my country haunt me with frequent and melancholy regret this you may term fantastical, but untrue or true to you, I tell you it is real with me   But, oh ' you will but class it with the phantoms of a diseased mind, however,

this is my protestation, believe or disbelieve it, regard it with thoughtful compassion, or with uncomprehending contempt, this is what I feel, and all that I feel, even as I feel it   *   *   *   *
I have renounced all the pleasures of society this may be condemned by you as frivolous, but bear in mind that our tastes are as different as our complexions, and that while you care not in how profound a seclusion you live, I have qualities that adapt me peculiarly for society, and the desires that naturally prompt me to seek it, indeed, the two go together   *   *   *   *   We are not all made up of affections—we have intellects—and we have passions—and each and all should have their objects and their spheres of action, or the creature is maimed as for retorting to this, ‘ What need of intellectual converse have you not an affectionate husband and two sweet babies?" You might as well say to a man who told you he had no arms—Oh! no, but you have legs "   *   *

At that period, May, 1839, her determination to abandon her home seemed so firmly fixed, that I was reluctantly compelled to appeal to others, which I had never yet done, my domestic troubles, great as they were, had happily never been mentioned to any one, but now there seemed no way to prevent so painful and scandalous a catastrophe but by invoking the intercession of friends Hitherto, whenever she talked of leaving me, I had diverted her purpose by soothing kindness, forbearance, gentleness, and by offering no apparent opposition to her wishes, but begging her to defer her intention until she could reflect on it more calmly, or to leave it for some other occasion In this way I succeeded in changing her intention, but now I tried every thing in vain, and, as a last resort, I was forced to make known to others the nature and extent of my domestic unhappiness I did not unburden myself to my own family, because I knew their sympathies would naturally be awakened for me, and their feelings might as naturally be enlisted against her

I will here remark, that I have never, not even up to the time I am now writing detailed to my own family the history of my domestic misery they first became aware that difficulties existed, when these were made known to the society in which we lived, and not till then, it was Mrs Butler herself who first openly spoke of them, not only to her friends, but to my kindred, whose impressions have all been received from her.

As I had failed in all my efforts to change her purpose, and as she was resolved upon an immediate departure, there was no time to write to England, to seek from her family and friends there the assistance I needed, and I applied to those in this country in whom she most confided The letters which passed between myself and these persons on that occasion are here inserted

"*Near Philadelphia, May* 31, 1839

"My dear Mrs Sedgwick,

" Yourself and your husband are the only persons to whom I dare speak of my misery, and open my domestic sorrows and trials I know that your regard for me and mine is sincere, and I know that my affection for you is true. To you then alone can I turn, and from you alone can I hope for comfort. * * * *

Think what I have suffered, for five years have I pent up in my breast and concealed from all a sorrow that destroyed almost all happiness My own family are as little aware of it as persons who never heard our name They think, as all who know me, that my life is passing quietly and smoothly, and that no cares but ill health have troubled me even my servants do not know that from the day I entered the church to swear love, faith, and constancy to one alone, that my life has been a tumult, I have concealed it from all and now for the first time do I make known to any one that unhappiness which it has been the object—almost the sole object—of my life for five years to avert I have done all that deep love for a wife, the strongest affection for my children and an earnest desire to secure peace and happiness for myself and them have dictated, but all has failed, and now I am forced to seek the aid of you my distant friends, to avert domestic misery and calamity, which would wreck the happiness of four persons for life You know our history as well almost as ourselves, that it was deep, true, free, and well tried love which caused us to marry, no selfish feeling, no thought of interest, indeed, no thought or feeling but that our mutual happiness and our fates were linked together, ever lodged in our breasts And so it is still At least it is so with me, and I think also with her I have never doubted the continuance and strength of her love for me and she should never have doubted mine I know that our feelings are as strong as when first we loved, but cemented and made holy by the birth of our two children And yet her life is passed in bitter misery in constant tears, and heart breaking sobs For nearly three years after our marriage we were never apart, no separation, not even of a day, occurred between us, until she went with Sarah to England, during that time various causes were assigned for her unhappiness, but chiefly being separated from her family and friends Lately, and only lately, has she taken up the idea that she has become indifferent to me, this arose I think in Georgia, and now has full possession of her mind. With all but me she is rational at all times, her care and management of our children are admirable, we have never once disagreed about them. But she will not live in

F

peace or quiet with me   It seems as if her spirit became troubled by my presence and would never settle down but like a boiling spring which rises out of the earth it is always troubled and agitated, and most uneasy is it when we are most together and alone   Oh! how anxiously I have tried to soothe and calm this perturbed spirit, and to make her happy, but the spirit would never rest   Sometimes argument would lead to disagreement and throw her into that state when reason leaves her, this I have avoided as much as possible   again my opinions if at variance with hers would lead to the same painful result so that at one time I restrained myself from ever expressing an opinion before her   she then complained that I never told her my thoughts or feelings, and even silence worked upon her to madness   ·   ·   ·   ·   This state of mind sometimes last three or four days. during which she evinces the strongest feeling against me sometimes of anger, sometimes aversion.   Five or six times she has packed up all her clothes to leave me   Twice she has taken her jewels to Philadelphia and sold them in order to obtain money to travel   and I have had the mortification of going to buy them back once being obliged to pay a considerable sum to enable me to get them again   When in Georgia she resolved to leave me, packed up her trunks, left the children on St Simon's Island, without saying a word to them or the nurse, and came to the plantation near Darien to go away in the steamboat, as it happened, no boat was to start for three or four days, for two days she shut herself up in a room, lay on a bed, and refused to eat or drink, because it was my food she would have to eat, and she would touch nothing or receive nothing that belonged to me   *   *   *   *   After our conversation the morning you left us I determined to return home as frequently as my business would allow me, though I well knew that not my absence, but my presence, caused the trouble.   I have been home often since you went away but my coming has created no apparent gratification or pleasure, I went into town on Saturday morning and returned again in the evening . until

Monday I was not away from home, and she seemed in better spirits than usual, but what was my surprise when at breakfast on Monday morning she asked me when the next steam packet would sail for England, I said the Great Western was advertised for June 13th she then told me that she had fully made up her mind to return to England, and go on the stage to support herself, and if I would not take means to send her back she would write to engage her own passage as I refused to take any steps about it, I presume she has done it herself for she sent a letter to the post office, which she did not show me, and which I am inclined to think was to make inquiries about a passage The day after this was Tuesday, 28th the birthday of both our children, then two cousins came to pass the day with them, and Fanny seemed happy all day I hoped she had given up her strange purpose, but I was mistaken, at night I was left to sleep alone, and a note, which I here copy, was left on a table in the bed room

" 'I have at various times made ineffectual struggles to get released from the intolerable life I am leading you have always prevented my doing so, by urging upon me considerations of your happiness as I can no longer be deceived by assurances which your actions most plainly contradict, I now request once for all to be allowed to return to my own country and such friends as remain to me there God knows how bitter a life mine has been for sometime past. I cannot endure it any longer and will not You can never repair the injury which you have done me in marrying me, although you seem to think that your having done so is a sufficient compensation for all the privations which I feel though they are imperceptible to you I will not remain here to be your housekeeper your child's nurse, or what you make me that is still more degrading and revolting I beg you will take immediate means for my return to England, and have the kindness to let me know whether you mean to do so or not '

"Alas! poor Fanny, the bitterness and misery are of her own creating and mar my happiness as effectually as her own God knows how earnestly I have striven to make her happy and how readily I would now do any thing in the world to secure it, for I should also be sure of happiness myself But the difficulty is with herself, it is inherent, and unless she can be made sensible of this and summon resolution to overcome this morbid state of feeling, she will be miserable for life She is undermining her health by this constant gloom and weeping, her nerves are very materially affected already, and the tone of her mind, as regards herself, is sickly and unnatural I have copied the note, because her own words will convey to you a more correct knowledge of the unhappy state of her mind than all I can write When I instance the condition of other women, as compared with hers, women who have much to depress them, but yet bear up against all their troubles and show a cheerful spirit, she can always find circumstances in their lot which serve to lighten their condition, and alleviate their sufferings so as to enable them better to overcome their troubles, and generally concludes by making out her situation the hardest and most unsupportable and unmitigated of all her sex. This constant dejection and gloom, if not broken down and dispelled, will become after a time a mere habit, and imagined misery will be ever present, indeed it seems to me that most of it is habit even now.   *   *   *

*   *   *   * And this I know will be the case with Fanny, if there be not some cure made now of this disease of the mind, the disease will master her and when at last she does perceive the true nature of it, it will be too late, for it will then be incurable. That she must feel very much the seclusion in which we live, and constantly regret the separation from her family and early friends no one can doubt, but it is no remedy to be eternally weeping and bemoaning this as the greatest and only calamity. She says that as she is not happy, and as I evidently am not, a separation had better take place. now it is not an easy matter to talk with

persons who are irrational and take wrong views of a case, and she talks of a separation as if we were two persons who had entered into partnership to carry on some small retail business, and not the great business of life—the lives not only of ourselves but of our children   If two marry and have no children, if love dies, and dislike grows up, if respect changes into disgust, if tempers are unsuited, if life is wasting away useless and unprofitable, and if the happiness of both can be secured by dissolving that tie which has been formed by such holy vows, and which should be so sacred—why let them part   But such are not we   If we are not happy together, more unhappy should we be apart   And do we not surely owe more, or rather are we not more bound to consider our children than ourselves?   And what would our children not lose by being bereft of their mother's guardian care?   What could I do with two little motherless children?   And would Fanny be happy parted forever from those darling children, earning her support by public show, even though she should be among her family and early friends?   But to one who has her reason the mere suggestion of a separation, situated as we are, must appear like madness.   With every means of happiness given to us, it is worse than foolish, it is sinful, wantonly to cast it aside   I think that I have done every thing in my power to render Fanny's situation comfortable, happy, and contented, I cannot, it is true, live in England, to enable her to be always with her family and friends there, but I have once afforded her an opportunity of visiting them, and passing nine months with them, and I look forward to going there again   If, however, she cannot be happy away from them, if a home, a husband and children, are less to her than former friends, and do not compensate for what she has given up, why there is nothing to be done, if unceasing tears are to be shed for those in England.—if they are dearer than all that belongs to her in this country, I fear there is no remedy   But if it remains for me to do yet more, if any thing is wanting on my part, if I can by any thing within my power secure a cheerful and contented home, which, alas, I have never known, only let me know it that at once it may be done   There is no one whose words would have any weight with her but yours and Mr Sedgwick's, her affection for you is very great, and she has so great an admiration of your character and understanding, that she would feel there must be truth in what you would tell her respecting herself and her situation   Besides she sees in you, and it is what we often speak of, the attainment of perfect and rational happiness in married life. What I say to her has no effect whatever   she always replies that I cannot realize her situation, and consequently do not make sufficient allowances for her   I tell her that human happiness depends not so much on outward circumstances as on ourselves, if we have but moderate means allowed us, we can attain the rest ourselves   this truth she will not allow

" You must not for a moment suppose that I complain. If I had no other object in writing to you, I should be silent altogether. It is because Fanny is wasting her health, her strength and her life in miserable dejection and morbid despondency that I seek relief, and I know not where to turn but to you our friends   How this present trouble will end I cannot see   heretofore there has been more passion and violence, at times, when she talked of leaving her home, and I have had to bring her back to reason and to her natural feelings by gentle kindness and soothing affection, begging her not to desert me and her children   On those painful occasions too she was determined to go out of the house at once, refusing either to sleep or eat under my roof again   But now it is different, as you will perceive by the tone of her note   She seems resolved to part, and asked me if I would allow her either of the children   I know not what to do   There is no one in this country to whom I would mention a word of this but yourselves   I have thought it right, therefore, indeed I felt bound to lay open every thing to you. for if she does leave me, her nearest friends ought to know under what circumstances she does so   If she persist in going, and I am unable to restore reason by my own endeavours, I will try to induce her to take the children and go to see you before leaving the country If she will agree to do this, I shall feel quite safe, and know that she will come back to me better and happier after having been with you * * * * I feel the necessity of making a strong effort at this time to prevent the recurrence of this state of mind, and to create a healthy and vigorous action of both mind and body, for if it be neglected the period will come when it cannot be done I am sure I need not say anything about writing my domestic troubles to you, my dear friends I know you will be pained by this letter, but if you can afford any aid—and it is because I believe you can that I write—I also know that you will rejoice, and not mind sharing with me my griefs If any change should take place, I will write to you.

"Your sincere friend,

"PIERCE BUTLER"

[Lenox] "*Thursday evening, June 6, 1839.*
"My dear Mr Butler,

"I have received, this evening, your most touching and painfully interesting letter, but am prevented by a room full of company from answering it as I wish I could do, without delay To-morrow I will write, if possible, to both of you—certainly to Fanny—and to you, immediately after I have considerable faith that I may induce her to forego this dreadful purpose Meanwhile, pray do not refrain from going home, under the idea that she is worse with you than without you. * * * * On the contrary, I think you should be at home as much as you can, certainly every night Try to recollect that she is diseased, and treat her soothingly and compassionately, as you would do if she were sick with an ordinary malady. She is morbidly susceptible to reproof, or disapprobation, and for the present, at least you must bear and forbear I have not yet had an opportunity to show my husband your letter, but you need not doubt that you will have his entire sympathy. I write in great haste and in a din of voices.

"God guide and comfort you.

"Most sincerely, your friend,

E. B. SEDGWICK."*

"*Lenox, June* 7, 1839

"My dearest Fanny,

"I have been exceedingly distressed by a letter which I received last evening from your husband, informing me of your dreadful purpose of leaving him, and begging that I will use my influence to dissuade you from it. In doing so, I shall feel that I am pleading for yourself as well as for him and the children. I have been thinking a great deal about you, dear Fanny, ever since I left you, and the more I have thought, the more I have turned over in my mind the subject of your troubles, the more I have viewed it in all its aspects, the stronger has my conviction become, that your mind is positively and greatly diseased, and that you have yourself been the cause of all that appearance of indifference in your husband which you now believe to be the original source of your unhappiness. I recollect saying to you a year ago when I was in Philadelphia, at the time he came home after staying in Philadelphia, when he was ill ·Fanny, my husband would die, if I should give him such a reception, after his being away—particularly under such circumstances,' and you replied 'Oh! he knows me perfectly well, he knows that when I feel most, I express least.' Still, I was not at all satisfied, because there is no strength of conviction that can counteract the effect of manners, as you have abundantly experienced in your own case. And when I came to speak upon the subject, with your husband, which I did when we drove into town the day I left Philadelphia, I found that it was exactly as I had supposed—that he staid away a

great deal—exiled himself in a measure, from his home, his wife and
his children, because his coming always made you unhappy, and
your greeting consisted in tears and sobs and sleepless misery And,
do you think, my dear Fanny, that with all that calmness of exterior he has not suffered deeply, intensely ? You know the power he
has of concealing his feelings and his inclination to do so, but the
sorrow has been secretly working till it has affected as I believe,
the fountain of life itself, and I should not be surprised if the catastrophe which now threatens him, in this desperate determination of
yours were to prove, ultimately, a death blow   I was speaking to
my husband, since I came home this spring, upon the effect your
husband's visits produced upon you to which he replied, that 'if it
were his case, he never should go home again in the world—he could
not ' I wish I could show you your husband's letter or rather, I
wish he would write just such a one to you, and lay open his whole
heart upon this subject   Think, dear Fanny, of the extremity of
misery which must have induced him to lay open the secrets of his
heart, and let one, who is comparatively a stranger, meddle there-
with, and, if he is indifferent to you, whence comes this racking
misery ? My dearest Fanny, believe me, you are altogether morbid
on this subject   You have the best means of happiness that this
world ever furnishes in your power, and still you are wretched
You have affluence a husband whose love you do not question, as
fine children as mortal was ever blessed with, and rare gifts of mind
and heart, but you inherit undoubtedly, from your mother those
morbid tendencies which poison and spoil all and if instead of manfully resisting them, of calling in the aid of religion, and of that
moral and intellectual strength for which you are remarkable you
yield to them, let them obtain this complete triumph over you, I
very much fear they will forever have the mastery   And what
think you, my dear friend, you will gain ? Because your husband is
the dearest object of your affections, to whom you look as the chief
source of your earthly happiness, you very naturally impute to him

F

all your want of happiness   But did not you tell me once, that you
admired Kate's discernment in telling you that she did not believe
you could be very happy in any situation?   And, surely, surely you
will find it so   Do you think, my dear Fanny, that England, or
English friends, or English society could make you happy for a single moment?   O no, no, believe me   I assure you there are those
things in every married woman's life which, if she were constituted
as you are, would make her as wretched as you   *   *   *
But, my dearest Fanny, even if you still persist in your belief, that
you are a wronged and injured woman, although your convictions
may remain just the same, in spite of all I can say, still I do not
think that they afford the slightest justification for your leaving your
husband   You have undertaken to be his wife, and to fulfil towards
him the duties of that relation, and, whatever you may think of
your marriage contract as a legal form, you must regard yourself as
pledged in the sight of heaven to fulfil what you have undertaken.
You voluntarily put yourself in the way of becoming a mother, and
I cannot think of a more heinous offence against God and right, than
to cast off this duty   You have no right, my dear Fanny, to deprive your husband of his children, even with his consent, extorted
by this strange necessity   You have no right to deprive them of
either of their parents, you have no right to separate yourself from
them, and place it out of your power to train them up in the way in
which they should go   Your husband speaks with admiration of
your management and care of your children, you have an immense
trust reposed in you, think what it is to have such a soul as Sarah's
put into your keeping, and will you consign it to any chance care?
Will you throw it away from you, as a vexed child tosses away her
plaything?   And suppose that your husband permits you to take her,
can you enjoy her when she reminds you constantly of what he has
given up?   You could not possibly see his life blood taken from
him, drop by drop, because it would be all a perceptible, visible process, but can you do that which the other, that is so palpable, only

faintly shadows forth? Might not the child, by and by, reproach you for taking advantage of her early years, and separating her, without her permission, from her natural home, and her best friend, except yourself? And could you guard her against the effect upon her character which such a precedent in you might have? Could you hope that any relation, any duty in life could be associated in her mind with the idea of that permanency and stability without which all good, all virtue, is liable to be as transitory as the passing shadow? My poor, dear Fanny, my precious, almost idolized friend, do let me persuade you that your mind is diseased How can you do this great iniquity, and sin against God? If, indeed, a mind in such a state as yours is morally responsible You have, dear great confidence in me, in my sense of right so much that I have sometimes wondered how I came to inspire it, but, since it is so, do put yourself under my guidance for a little time do not act rashly, hastily give yourself time to consider of all that I have said to you come and pass some time in Lenox, come directly Attend to your health, let nature's sweet influences minister to you, and enjoy the love of those who, because they do not excite so intense a feeling in you as your husband, are best fitted to comfort and soothe you I have written in greatest haste Let me hear from you very soon, I pray, and once more, I pray you do not take this desperate measure, now, at any rate. You would be ready to cast yourself into the sea, the moment that you saw the shore receding God guide and bless and comfort you

"Your most true and loving,

"E B S"*

"*Lenox, June* 7, 1839

"My dear Mrs Butler,

"Do not leave your husband, I pray you for God's sake It cannot be right—at any rate, it cannot *now* If you had less mind, less

---

* Mrs Charles Sedgwick

heart, less feeling, so that you could view this matter as affecting yourself alone, it would be different   Believe me, you will feel remorse, and that, that is the only thing you *cannot* bear   You will have strength for every thing else, but not for this   Think, think of your own experience, of the bitter sufferings you have felt, and perhaps inflicted by a thought, a word, an action, the result of accident caprice, bodily infirmity, perhaps, or sudden passion   Think how your life has been poisoned, and that of those you love, by a look of coldness or a word in anger, so that the whole past and future has been swallowed up in one bitter feeling of the intolerable present   Have you made no mistake as to the cause of your sufferings? Have not some of the most intense been the most transient? Is it possible that the remedy you propose will avail you? It is impossible
*   *   *   *   But suppose you could have an abiding conviction that both you and Pierce could be as happy when separated as you are capable of being, would that justify you in taking a step against his most earnest wish and prayer, the consequences of which you cannot foresee, and which is irretrievable   *   *

' For his sake, for yours, and your children's, for the sake of my sister and daughter and wife, for the sake of all who love you and trust in you, do not yield to your present feelings, they will not last   Wait, and know that your extraordinary powers are given to you for an infinitely higher purpose than self-tormenting—not to shut yourself up in a cave of despair, but to pour the light of love and knowledge into the dark places of sin and ignorance

" God bless you

'Yours most affectionately.

"CHAS SEDGWICK."

Immediately after reading these excellent letters from Mr and Mrs Sedgwick, I addressed the following to Mrs Butler, which, at a subsequent period, returned into my possession

" My own dear Wife

" Will you consider well every word that our good friends have written you, it is most wise counsel, and for your own sake, every word ought to be impressed on your memory and heart, you should not say that you will endeavour to overcome the morbid state of your mind but you should say I will do it and like a drunkard who dashes forever from his lips the bitter cup that has brought wretchedness on himself and his family you should summon strong resolution, and never again allow yourself to fall into that state in which reason leaves her seat I was forced to seek aid from others, because you never heeded what I told you, and always became irritated when I suggested that your unhappiness was not caused by real, but by sickly and imaginary griefs I therefore begged those friends, in whom you have both confidence and affection, to use their influence to restore your mind to a healthy tone It is by no means pleasant to have to tell persons of their faults or defects, because few can feel that the censure is just and if I attempt to point out some of those which I think cause you much unhappiness, it is neither in the spirit of complaint nor of censure, but that you may, if possible, avoid them and if I did not know that you have it in your power to drive them from you entirely, I would say nothing about them Think of what our life has been, when we have been at home quietly and peacefully, with nothing real to disturb us and when we ought and might have been happy and contented Has our home ever been a cheerful one? Think of the tears that have been shed for self-created griefs, and the gloom that has reigned over our house, until it was almost a house of mourning, with nothing to cheer or brighten the domestic scene but the blessed spirits of our darling child and if you can realize the gloomy period as it has been, think if it is not imperious to break down these self-conjured barriers to our happiness It is singular that the fate of your unfortunate mother does not act as a warning, and that the sad example she gave has not been shunned, one who, as your friend Mr Harness de-

scribes her, 'possessed such high gifts of nature, and such abundant
means of conferring happiness on others and receiving it herself, yet
who marred the blessing to those she loved the most, and emptied
her own breast of it' And Mrs Sedgwick tells you, 'that you
have the best means of happiness in your power that this world ever
furnishes, and still you are wretched And with rare gifts of mind
and heart, you inherit from your mother those morbid tendencies
which poison and spoil all, and if instead of manfully resisting
them, of calling in the aid of religion and of that moral and intellectual strength for which you are remarkable, you yield to them, and
let them obtain this complete triumph over you, I very much fear
they will forever have the mastery' And Mr Sedgwick says to
you, 'know that your extraordinary powers are given to you for an
infinitely higher purpose than self-tormenting' And I beseech you,
oh, my beloved wife, to turn over a new page and commence a clear
and bright era in our mutual existence, one in which no clouds, no
gloom, no unhappiness, shall ever come Never doubt the strength
and continuance of my affection for you—that can never cease. It
is true you have it in your power to make me unhappy, to cause my
home to be distasteful to me and to force me away from you and
my children—but you cannot make me cease to love you You
cannot drive me to seek pleasure or enjoyment away from you, if I
cannot have happiness in my own home, it is no where for me. I
may not be happy with you, but oh, most true it is, that I cannot
be happy without you If sobs and tears are my welcome when I
return to my home, and if I am left to lie alone in my bed while you
pass the night on the floor absorbed in grief, it can hardly be expected that I shall find my home a cheerful one, nor can it be wondered at if I should sometimes absent myself from a home where
gloom so often prevails, which heretofore my coming has never dispelled, but it is not true to say that indifference either to you or my
children has ever kept me away from you Fanny, my own Fanny,
I feel in my heart that but one calamity can ever happen to me in

this life, which would make me hopelessly wretched, and from which I could never recover, if you or my children were to be taken from me by death. I could never be happy again   But if you are spared to me, and only seem happy, I may defy all else, for indeed I have always felt that I had fortitude to bear up against all the worst ills of life, but your loss   Then, dear wife, drive from your mind the false and base idea that you have become indifferent to me— it is not so   There is no joy for me in this life no happiness, no comfort not derived from you and my children, or which springs from any other source whatever   Then resolve, with that powerful resolution which you possess, that henceforth you will make the best use of all those means of happiness which surround us, and not wantonly squander those riches which you have, merely because you cannot attain yet greater riches.   Oh think what a priceless jewel pure affection is, and how it should be treasured in our hearts, how carefully we should guard it, and ' suffer not a breath to dim the bright gem's purity '   Oh! my wife be wise '"

It was my intention again to visit Georgia, and to take my family there with me to pass the winter of 1839–40   Having this in view we left home about the beginning of December, and came into Philadelphia, preparatory to our southern journey   While in the city we at all times stayed with my brother, whose house was to me and mine the same as my own   Mrs Butler was invariably treated with consideration and kindness by my brother and his wife, and my children received from them the same affection as their own daughter   While there I was taken ill, and remained so for nearly two months, nor was it until the end of January, 1840, that I found myself able to leave Philadelphia   Thus, instead of the few days originally expected and planned, we were detain-

ed in town much longer During this time, the greater part of which I was ill and suffering, Mrs Butler
exhibited the same irregularities of temper and unrea-
sonableness of conduct that marked her life at all
other times One day she was going out to ride on
horseback, which she generally did unattended just
before starting she said to me, that she would ride
down Walnut street to the river Delaware and go
along the wharves, as she wished to become more acquainted with the city, I begged her not to ride in
that direction, as ladies never went along the wharves
at any time, and that a lady going there on horseback
and alone, would attract great if not rude attention,
and cause unpleasant remarks to be made, she replied
by a few disdainful words about my regard for what
people said dashed off, and took her ride along the
wharves This is only one of the many instances of
perverse self-will, in which she delighted

Other similar proceedings of hers at this time, are
recorded in her own letters and I insert them as
characteristic specimens of complaints, utterly groundless and fanciful The following is from herself to
her father

Philadelphia, Tuesday, January 7th, 1840

My dearest Father,

"I little thought at the time of my marriage, that the proceeds of
my professional exertions would ever be *necessary* to my comfort,
and yielded them to you for my mother's and your use, with no
thought or desire but that they had been more You will, I dare
say, be both surprised and grieved when I tell you, that the small
income which I could derive from that sum of money, would greatly
contribute to my positive comfort and that of my children From

circumstances which I do not by any means understand myself, but of which the results are sufficiently intelligible, I find myself and my children living upon Mr John Butler I have neither home nor servants of my own, and as far as I can ascertain from my husband, whose sole reply to my inquiries is that this matter is his business, he cannot afford to place me or his children in any other situation I have determined under these circumstances, to resume my profession for to be dependent for the means of living upon comparative strangers is contrary alike to my feelings and principles, and my reason for addressing this letter to you, is to beseech you, if you have not borne in mind your promise to me, that the money I gave up to you at my marriage should revert to me hereafter to do so henceforth for indeed I know not what my need of it may be I write hurriedly and in great distress of mind, many most painful reflections crowding upon me at once God bless you, my dearest Father, I hope to see you soon and am ever, ever,

"Your affectionate child

"FANNY BUTLER"

This letter was sent to me by Mrs Butler, for my perusal, accompanied by the following to myself

"*January 7th*, 1840

" You have often evaded questions, which as they concerned *myself*, I had a right to make, you now tell me that the situation in which I am placed is your business and not mine I have determined, and nothing shall alter my determination, that since you refuse to discharge your duty to me I will no longer be dependent upon you, the implicit confidence and trust I had in you has been shaken, you have broken the contract which should have existed between us, for you have concealments from me, and I *can* no longer rely upon you My comfort and happiness are as you say your business, but, as like most other of your business, you neglect them

G

utterly, I will so far see to them myself, that I will no longer submit to live upon your relations. I have asked you for what I have a right to, for I can obtain it for myself, a home, no matter how poor, how humble, where I might live with my children in decent privacy and by myself, a home where if I have neither kindred nor friends of my own, at least I shall not be dependent upon strangers, upon whom you have thrust me without regard for either my feelings or theirs. I do not wonder that you care little for these, however, for you are regardless of the dearest interest of your children, you have subjected them to inconvenience of every description, and what is far, far worse, to pernicious moral influences,* without thought, care, or consideration. I give you my solemn word of honour that I will live thus no longer, and if you do not choose to give me the justice which I have a right to claim, I will resort to the means which, I thank God, I possess of maintaining myself, without depending either upon your careless discharge of your duties, or upon the sufferance of your relations."

Having retained a copy of Mrs Butler's letter to her father, I returned it to her with the following remonstrance —

'*January* 10*th*, 1840.

"I return your letter to your father, but I earnestly warn you against sending it to him. It is untrue it is most unjust, it belies me to your family, who are at a distance, which makes it impossible for them to know the truth, it was written in temper, it will be treating your family most unkindly to send such an account to them,

---

* At the time that Mrs Butler made this wanton and shameless imputation "of subjecting my children to pernicious moral influences,' they were little more than infants, their ages being four and a half and one and a half years respectively and we were living as transient travellers in my brother's house, where they had a nursery to themselves, their own nurse to attend upon them, and every possible kindness and attention

for it will grossly deceive them as to your real situation If you
send it, you will regret it before it has probably left the country, for
your better feelings will prevail over those which now possess you,
and you will feel the injustice of what you have done If you write
any thing else, I entreat to be allowed to see it, I have a right to
make this request, whatever you write concerns me more nearly
than yourself for it goes to those who know you, but who know me
only through you "

Those who know nothing of the way in which my
brother and myself lived, will find it difficult to believe that the state of things portrayed in her two
preceding letters existed only in Mrs Butler's own
discontented and distorting mind but all our ac-
quaintances—I make not a solitary exception—and
indeed most persons in Philadelphia well know how
strikingly untrue, how utterly void of the semblance
of truth, are her representations

In consequence of being kept at the north so far
into the winter, I gave up the intention of taking my
family with me to the south, and at the beginning of
February, 1840, I went to Georgia without them.
At the same time Mrs Butler and the children returned to our own home

The following letters were written from home by
her to me shortly after my departure It must be
admitted that they contain quite sufficient disproof
and recantation of the extraordinary assertions contained in the letter to her father, namely, that she had
"neither home nor servants of her own," and that
she was "dependent for the means of living upon
comparative strangers "

Philadelphia, Thursday, Feb 13, 1840

"My dear Pierce,

"You probably imagined, after your last Saturday's plunge into the positive fact of departing, that you had at all events gained something by the effort, some relief from thought, consideration, and responsibility, some respite from domestic duties and household annoyances. Your slavery, doubtless you thought to leave on *this* side of Mason and Dixon's line, and looked not to be pestered with 'arrangements' even to the very bank of the Altamaha. I am heartily sorry that it cannot be so, and still more sorry to be the person perpetually doomed to the hateful office of 'sweet remembrancer!'

"We all came home to day, and even after a few hours the house begins to wear its accustomed aspect, the children are snug in bed, and I, as usual, in lonely grandeur in the drawing room. I came out on horseback, the roads were very muddy, and Forrester was one mass of mire almost to his girths. When I got here, Francis, who had gone to town with the wagon for the trunks, had not returned. Thomas was in town also and there was nobody but little Johnny Little to stable my steed, or to throw a blanket over him
*   *   *   *   Sarah is well, but little Fanny is by no means so, she has a bad cough and cold, and looks pale, I am thankful to have her once more at home. Pray answer me immediately about this and believe me,

"Ever your affectionate wife,

"FANNY "

"*Philadelphia, Tuesday, March* 3, 1840

"My dearest Pierce,

*   *   *   *   "Your children are very well; Fanny has had not the slightest symptom of croup since our return to the country, though she has been out every day, and almost all day long, her appearance is much more healthy lately, and she

seems altogether happy and well   ·   *   *   *

Last week I had Mackintosh, Mary, Fanny Appleton, then maid, Kate Bowie, her maid, and her little boy, all in the house at once Kate and her child had been staying with me a few days, when the Highlander and his clan appeared, they arrived last Sunday week, and staid until the Thursday following, don't you wonder how I packed them? Kate Bowie and her baby had the nursery, her maid the next room, and Fanny Appleton the little third room, on that side I gave up my room to Mackintosh and Mary, and slept with Sarah on the blue sofa-bed in my dressing-room, with baby's crib beside it, and our children were washed and dressed in your dressing-room, and the gentle Marianne, Mary's maid was exalted to an attic There all went as I told you, last Thursday, but Kate and her child are still with me   ·   *   *

Ella and Lizzy, and Mary and Alfred (the boy) come out and spend every Saturday with me   ·   ·   * |

' I grieve to hear of your low spirits, though its some relief to me to think that I am not now near you to wear and harass you, and produce the depression you complain of   ·   ·   *   *
God bless you

' Ever your own

" WIFE."

" Philadelphia Thursday, March 19, 1840

" My dearest Pierce,

*   ·   ·   *   " We are all here most anxious and unhappy about you, for me I am almost in despair, I thought that once freed from the gloom and disquietude which my thrice unhappy temperament seems to throw over you, and alone with John[*] in that favourable climate, you would have at least a temporary relief from pain and depression Oh! my dearest, what can be done for you!

* My brother

Will you not do something for yourself, why do you not go to Europe, to Germany, and try the efficacy of those waters, but above all, the efficacy of change of scene, of pleasurable excitement, and of absence from all depressing influences   John would go with you too gladly and as for me, I should too gladly see you go in the pursuit of health, and that once cheerful and blessed equanimity of temper and spirits which was your most peculiar and fortunate possession   ·   ˘   ⁄   ⌐   God bless you, my darling dearest Pierce, when you think of me—*if* you think of me—think of me as one whose love for you has been a source, not of joy or delight, but of pain and agony, and now of bitter reproach, for oh! Pierce, Elizabeth* has written me some of the contents of that letter of yours to her, and I felt while reading it as if the iron was indeed entering my soul, forgive me, my dearest, dearest Pierce, if I have so bitterly cursed your existence   I cannot write any more, I am blinded with crying

> "Ever, ever your own wife,

> "FANNY"

At that time, and while I was still in Georgia, I received the following letter from Mrs Charles Sedgwick —

> "*Lenox, March* 31, 1840

' My dear Friend,

"Do I incur the risk of being stigmatized as a meddler by writing to you again upon matters with which a stranger may not intermeddle? I will not think so, because I know you are fully aware how much I have at heart yours and Fanny's mutual happiness, and will therefore believe that I act from the deepest and most sincere interest in you both   I have, besides, your own sanction, for, in that long letter which you wrote me last spring, you said, 'But if it remains

---

* Mrs Charles Sedgwick

for me to do yet more; if any thing is wanting on my part, if I can by any thing within my power, secure a cheerful and contented home, only let me know it, that at once it may be done' I anny says she has written to tell you how far I had lately betrayed your confidence and therefore it is better that I should mention why I had been induced to betray it at all if, indeed, that is the proper term to use She was very eager that I should show her the letter last summer, and wished me to obtain your permission to that effect I thought it would have been much better that she should see it and the only reason I did not comply with her request was that by introducing the subject I might seem to take advantage of the confidence which you had voluntarily reposed in me in a moment of extremity You know that she is in the habit of opening her whole heart to me, and, of course, she wrote to me, how wretched she was all the time she was in Philadelphia   *   *   *

It was about the same time, and before I answered this letter, that she wrote me how much you were suffering since your arrival in Georgia with low spirits, and how much she lamented your being made to endure an evil from which, hitherto, you had been so completely, though so strangely exempt I replied, that I was astonished at her imagining that you had never been unhappy I alluded to what you must necessarily have suffered from all her discontent and wretchedness, and quoted, in proof of it a little sentence from your letter. I took occasion, at the same time, to say how inconsiderate and how wrong I thought she had been in indulging so much, and manifesting, so openly, those feelings which had caused you both so much sorrow Now as I presume you have found out from her letters, she is overwhelmed with remorse, and all her tenderness for you is again at full tide It is strange that the idea of her ever having made you unhappy seems to be an entirely new revelation to her I have besought her, as now permit me to beseech you, my dear friend, that, henceforth, you may know each others hearts completely If she had known that she was making you so unhappy, the circumstance would have been of the greatest possible assistance to her, I am sure, in checking and controlling the feelings that have had the mastery of her to her own hurt, and your great sorrow. And now I have it deeply at heart that the present moment should be improved for setting all matters right between you, that each of you should henceforth see and perform his duty to the other Even without any personal interest in the matter, I should most deeply lament the waste of such rich such abundant, such precious materials for happiness as are in your hands   *   ,   *   *

"God bless you, my dear friend, and may you both hereafter be as happy, as, with love such as you have for each other you surely may be

' Yours, truly and affectionately,

' E B Sedgwick.

"Pierce Butler Esq , *Darien Georgia* '

After passing three months in the south, I returned to the north, in May, 1840, and joined Mrs Butler and my children at home We resided there, with occasional absences, until November, in the same year At that time Mrs Butler received letters from her friends in England, representing her father's health to be very precarious, and advising her, if she expected ever to see him again, to lose no time in reaching England Our decision was quickly made in exactly one week from the receipt of those letters, namely, on the first of December 1840, we sailed from New York, in the steamship British Queen We landed at Southampton on the twenty-first of December, and the next day went to London

ABROAD.

~~~~~~~~

M<small>R</small> K<small>EMBLE</small>'s disease had attained a crisis he was
scarcely alive, and was expected to sink at every hour
For some days there was no apparent change he only
breathed the hopes of his most sanguine friends did
not look to his restoration But he revived life
seemed to come back to him by slow degrees, and,
contrary to the fears of all, he recovered

He was relieved of active disease at the time of our
coming, but his illness had lasted so long, and had
been so severe, that the worst was hourly apprehend-
ed The arrival and presence of his daughter, no
doubt, contributed to, if it did not actually cause, his
resuscitation

At that time Mr Kemble did not keep house in
London we found him at lodgings As soon as he
was able to leave his bed we took a furnished house
and resided together

When I left home I had no intention of staying
away longer than a few months, my absence was pro-
tracted, however, to two and a half years We did
not return to the United States until May, 1843
The whole of this time, with the exception of occasional visits to other places, was passed in London

H

Our social position there was a most agreeable and
fortunate one Mr Kemble had passed a long, dis-
tinguished and respected life he had hosts of friends.
friends of the best sort, of the highest classes in life,
and of long tried constancy They were rejoiced at
his recovery they appreciated the filial affection
which brought his daughter across the Atlantic to see
him in his illness, and they showed to him to her.
and to myself all the kindness and attention in their
power

If any condition of life, or concurrence of circumstances could have rendered Mrs. Butler contented
and satisfied she ought to have been wholly so during
our visit together to her native country The many
excellent friends I had there, and nearly all my ac-
quaintances, were made through her and her family,
and, consequently, they were her friends even more
than mine, and, from the day of our arrival to that of
our departure, their kindness never remitted

Those of my countrymen who travel rapidly through
England, or do not reside in it as I did, can know little of the real nature of its people The inhabitants
of every country have some peculiarity of character
one belonging to the English is coldness of exterior,
reserve towards those whom they casually meet, and
do not know From this, it is often thought by strangers among them, that they lack warmth and depth of
feeling, but you must not judge an Englishman out
of his house, you must see him in it Let him once
invite you to his fireside, and it will be your own, not
his insensibility, if you do not find yourself there
again and again London is a vast place a stranger

might live in it for a life-time without making a single acquaintance, but let one go there with a proper introduction, and he will see the icy surface at once dissolved, and hearts and houses open to him   Such was, undoubtedly, my happy experience   I was led also to observe that an American carries into English society a surer passport than any other foreigner, it is much easier for him, if made known to them reliably, to win a welcome even to their most exclusive circles than it is for a stranger from another land they are cordial in their reception of him, and sincere in their desire to show him all hospitable attention It may be, I shall never again be among them, but the recollection of their unvarying kindness is ever present to me, and the warmth of my feelings to them can never be chilled

In April, 1841, Mrs Butler's sister and aunt returned from Italy, and they also resided with us Her two brothers, not resident in London, came frequently to make short stays with us   Thus at length, she was in the position she had so often sighed for when in America she was in her own country she had husband, children, father, sister, brothers relations, friends, all around   Was she satisfied? Yes, for a time, while the excitement and novelty of her situation lasted, but no longer as the sequel unfortunately made too manifest

We passed the summer of that year, 1841, in travelling in Germany, and returned to London in October   Some time after our return, the occurrence happened which has been spoken of at page 15, namely. the application from America to contribute

an article for an anti-slavery newspaper   This seemed suddenly to set the old leaven of discontent to
work afresh   She now practically maintained the
principle, always contended for, of doing exactly as
she chose   Having yielded one point, she seemed to
think herself specially justified in persisting on all
others, and she assumed the attitude of opposition
and resistance to my wishes, never afterwards abandoned

The first time that she actually deserted me in
England was in April, 1842   No particular circumstance could be assigned as the cause of her abandonment, other than a recurrence of her moral disease
She apprized me by note, that her design was to return to America and added   "I have full confidence,
"that rather than see me return to the stage to earn
"my subsistence, you will allow me sufficient for my
"maintenance (I care not how little), till my father
"dies, when I hope you will be freed from the charge
"of me" She packed up all her clothing and left London by the railway for Liverpool, on the morning of
April 4th   I followed in hasty pursuit, by the next
train of cars and overtook the one in which she had
started, at Birmingham, here both trains united, and
we went on together to Liverpool, arriving at 7 o'clock
the same evening

She proceeded immediately to the Adelphi Hotel,
sent for Mr Radley, the proprietor, and directed him
to engage a passage for her in the steamer, to sail the
next day for Boston   I went into her room to dissuade
her from her purpose, for several hours I pleaded in
vain, I represented to her the unaccountable appearance her sudden departure would have, leaving chil-

dren, family, and friends, without warning or farewell,
I spoke of her father's grief, and of the mortification
as well as distress, her sister and friends must un-
dergo but for a long time her resolution was un-
shaken At length, and after it was far into the night,
I promised her that if she deferred her voyage until
the next steamer only, and then was of the same mind,
I would attend her to America, and thus save the ex-
posure and pain to her family and myself for sometime she refused even this proposal, but finally acceded to it, and the next day she returned with me to
London

Mrs Butler's next desertion was on the 4th of
July, in the same year—1842 I was not warned of
her intention, but suspected it she sent for a hack
cab off a stand near the house, and went away I
noticed the driver, and when he returned to the stand,
questioned him as to whither he had gone he told
me to the Southampton Railway, where his fare had
taken a train of cars which was about starting on her
arrival I felt assured she had gone to her brother's
who lived about twenty miles from London, near
Weybridge, and whom we occasionally visited That,
however, was not her destination, she stopped at
Kingston, twelve miles from London. and staid at a
public hotel She wrote four or five lines to me from
that place the next day, requiring money, which would
support her until the theatre opened in September
following, when she intended going upon the stage
and supporting herself I sent her money, and after
an absence of three or four days she came back She
did not return, however, with the purpose of remain-

ing, but merely to get her wardrobe and take a fresh departure Finding her resolved, I proposed to her that she should take one of the children and go to Scotland, on a visit to some relatives and friends there She agreed, and after a few days she went to Edinburgh, accompanied by our elder daughter She wrote to me from that place —

> " *Mackay's Hotel, Princes Street,*
>
> " *Edinburgh, July* 29, 1842.

*   *   *   *   "I am now in Edinburgh with eight pounds sterling only in my purse, my sister is extremely urgent with me to go on with her to Carlisle and Liverpool, and Mrs. Henry Siddons equally pressing for me to go with her to North Berwick (three hours from Edinburgh), where she is staying with Colonel and Mrs Muir, and their children, for the sake of sea bathing I should like to do either very much, but am withheld by your having yourself fixed upon Edinburgh as the place where you thought I had better remain   *   *   *   *   I shall keep Sarah with me as long as you think proper that her lessons shall be interrupted, and shall remain here according to your desire until I hear that you no longer choose me to do so I suppose you will take some measures to supply me with money, without which, indeed, I can neither very well stay here, or go elsewhere I have not the least objection to returning to America with my children, and endeavouring to discharge my duty to them but wish in the meantime not to return to the house where you are, and when we return to take passage in some other vessel "   *   *   *   *

As she said it was her intention to remain in Edinburgh, I did not reply to her letter immediately , and before answering it, I went to Liverpool to see a mercantile house there with whom I had some business

to transact   There I found her sister, with her husband, Mr Sartoris, to whom she had been recently
married, and I stayed with them   As Mrs Butler
was not to leave Edinburgh, until she heard from me,
I was surprised by her arrival at the hotel in Liverpool   She coolly informed me, that not choosing to
remain any longer in Edinburgh, she had borrowed
fifty pounds sterling from a friend there, and had come
to Liverpool to join her sister

After being here a few days, she seemed to be
brought under the influence of better feelings towards
myself, and, through her sister, expressed a desire for
another reconciliation   I readily yielded to her proposal hoping as usual for a favourable change in her
conduct, and catching at every possibility to secure
domestic harmony and quiet   We accordingly returned together to London on August 17, and continued to live together for some time on better terms
than had existed for many months

I designed returning to the United States late in
the autumn of that year—1842   In view of this, about
the middle of November, I gave up the house which,
to that time, I had occupied in common with Mrs.
Butler's father and sister   Mr Kemble took lodgings
for himself, Mrs Butler's sister, Mrs Sartoris, went
to a house of her own, and I fixed my family at the
Clarendon Hotel   We lived at this hotel for five
weeks, during which I changed my intention of immediately returning to America and determined to
continue in London until the following spring   I engaged another house for the time I was to remain,
and we were about removing to it, when Mrs Butler

once more took to flight Her better feelings, which
had ruled for a time after our reconciliation at Liverpool, had all again deserted her, and my life was dis-
tracted and embittered by the violence of her cause-
less and ceaseless excitements In consequence of
some disagreement between us which took place late
one night, while we were still at the Clarendon, the
immediate origin of which I cannot now recal, she
became very extravagant in language and manner, and
said she would instantly go away It was near two
o clock at night, she rang the bell, which was answered
by the night porter she ordered him to fetch her a
cab, and he went to do so While he was gone, I
spoke to her in a tone equally distinct and decided, I
told her we had but one more day to stay where we
were, before leaving it for our own house, and that if she
was bent on departure she must at least postpone it
until we had left the hotel She persisted, however,
and I then said to her, if she did quit the hotel in
that disgraceful manner, at that hour of the night, I
would, on the morrow, take the children to Liverpool, sail for the United States in the first steamer,
and she should never see either of us again. At that
moment the porter announced the cab to be at the
door, I told him to send it away, as it would not be
wanted he did so, and she said nothing The next
morning, however, she left the hotel, and went to her
sister's The day after that I removed with my children to the house I had engaged

Some of her letters to me, written at that period in
London, have been published by Mrs Butler in her

"*Narrative*' These letters have been widely read and universally admired and they are certainly remarkable compositions Though addressed to me they were not written, as it would appear, exclusively for my eye, for copies of them were carefully taken at the time, shown to her friends preserved, and after a lapse of nearly six years displayed as evidence against me in a court of justice I do not object however, to this having been done but I will show that they have been made to play a part altogether disingenuous and neither honest nor truthful She says, in her '*Narrative* —' I long continued however de-"votedly attached to him, and earnestly desired and 'repeatedly manifested the desire to recover his affec-"tions and win back his regard In order more fully, "and by means of original memorials, to expose the "nature of my exertions and the habitual sufferings of "my life, I annex hereto, and desire leave to prove ' true and perfect copies marked Exhibits A B C "and D of certain letters addressed by me to him "during the period referred to '* And she continues, "These appeals on my part failed to produce any ef-"fect, and his indifference and unkindness continuing "to be habitual my happiness as a wife was wholly "destroyed" That these appeals failed to produce any effect on me, is not true The effect they produced was such, that a reconciliation was the consequence In her ' *Narrative*" Mrs Butler has placed these four eloquently finished compositions together as if

* The publication of these letters in her *Narrative* has necessarily compelled me to insert in this Statement some private correspondence, which under other circumstances, my feelings naturally would have deterred me from exposing

I

none others had intervened, and as if they had failed
to elicit answers from me while other letters of hers
written at the same time, and all my replies, are entirely omitted Of my replies I have unfortunately
retained no copies it was not my habit to copy what
I addressed to her, but on examining her letters to
me I have accidentally found among them the original
drafts of two of my answers, which I insert in their
proper order If I possessed all my replies, so that
they might be read in the connexion in which they
were written, these selected letters of hers would appear very differently, as may be judged from the tenor
of the two, which, by a fortunate chance, I am able
to present

The following letters passed between us while we
were residing at the Clarendon Hotel the first, from
Mrs Butler to me, is one that she has herself published, marked 'Exhibit A " in her " *Narrative* "

" My dear Pierce,

" The other day when I asked you what it was that you required
from me when you rejected the attempt at a reconciliation, that my
affection and conscience both prompted me to make, you replied,
that until I *obeyed your will*, you would not be reconciled to me
In reflecting most solemnly upon our sad condition, and the means
by which I may have been instrumental in causing it, and the means
(if any) by which I might, perhaps, ameliorate it, I have been at a
loss to imagine in what I have disobeyed your will, or opposed any
wish of yours, but with regard to the question which you asked me
about the money I had borrowed *this*, I believe,—I mean refusing
to answer that question,—is the only act of opposition to your will
with which I can tax myself At the time when I refused to satisfy you
upon that point, your mode of interrogating me was such as to rouse
all the worse feelings of my nature,—pride, resentment, and a resist-

ance which I conceived justified—to a demand which I thought you had no right to make. But I perceive that our position is so *perilous* now, our future happiness, more, much more, our future conduct, seems threatened at this moment by such fatal influences, that there is no possible concession of pride or resentment or any other feeling that I am not prepared to make for the sake of retrieving the past and averting the future. That future, do you see what it is?—do you contemplate as I do in it the utter destruction of all our hopes, the deterioration, it may be, the complete degradation of our characters? Look through the remainder of our youth, more than one half of which is now already past—at what lies before us—a home without love, without peace, without virtue, whence we shall each of us make haste to depart as from a place accursed, to seek forgetfulness of all its disappointments at bitter sources which will return nothing but poison into our hearts. Look further yet, to age, and think of the lonely present, the dark and accusing retrospect, the cheerless and fearful prospect which must close the existence of two human beings who have thus wickedly wasted every blessing that ever was bestowed upon creatures most favoured by Providence. For what a lot *might* ours be! Have we not youth—health—wealth—a most fortunate social position—many friends who love us and rejoice in our welfare—children—oh! Pierce!—Pierce! I look at our children and tremble, lest God should strike them for our sins, lest we should be punished in some awful way through them for our abuse of all the benefits which are daily showered upon us and which we are turning into judgments against ourselves. For God's sake and for your children's sake, and for your own soul's sake, Pierce! my husband, oh, still my most tenderly beloved, let us be wise before it is too late! Show me wherein I have sinned in this our terrible condition, and mercifully help me to amend it.

"Save yourself, Pierce, and me, and our darling children, from a ruin worse than any worldly beggary, from self-condemnation and condemnation of each other, from a daily and hourly departure further

and further from all noble and holy influences Let us be friends,
let us be Christians, let us return to our duties, and to the paths
where peace and happiness are found I implore you by that love
which you once had for me, by that unalterable love which I still
bear you and which makes me dread being the cause of wrong in
you, more than any conceivable thing put away from your heart all
evil thoughts and feelings towards me forgive me forgive me, and
deal with me with righteous and merciful dealing, and spare yourself
the reproaches of your conscience, and the upbraidings of your better
nature Do not for God's sake, give yourself up to unworthy pur
suits and pleasures remember your children, Pierce, and as you
hope to influence them towards what is noble, virtuous, and excellent do not forsake them and me, and destroy our common life,
which, if not one of sacred mutual duties of mutual help compassion
and affection, *must* be a thing accursed and evil to us all, which we
shall have to answer for having made so Before writing this to
you I prayed to God to grant that I might speak to your heart as I
have spoken from my own May He bless you and guide you and
enlighten you, my husband '

This letter, which contains apparently as much real
feeling as it does beautiful writing is one of those
which Mrs Butler asserts failed to produce any effect
on me That this assertion is untrue, will be proved
by the following reply given to it, but which she
has entirely suppressed This reply is taken from
my original corrected draft, which was accidentally
preserved, as before stated

' It is my most earnest desire to be reconciled to you, nothing can
be so miserable as the life we are now leading, unless, indeed, it was
the life we did lead previous to our separation if we are not more
happy now than then, at least in our present condition we are not in
that constant state of irritability towards each other, and so far we

are better off Much as I wish to be reconciled to you, and much as I am impelled to give way to the impulse of love and affection which attracts us mutually towards each other, we had better not do so, unless our union is to be permanent, and unless our future mode of life is to be different from the past This can only be the result of a clear understanding of the terms upon which we are to live together in future We have frequently had differences and quarrels during the time that we have lived together we have several times parted from each other, and as often been brought together again by the strong bond of love which first attracted us to each other, and which I firmly believe is as strong now as ever it was, but our reunions heretofore have resulted in a temporary happiness only, after a short lull the same old grievances have given rise to the same unhappy and miserable differences between us, so that indeed with few intervals our whole married life has been a troubled existence, disturbed by contentions and disputes. This must not be so for the future either we must live apart, wretched as such a life is for ourselves and unfortunate and injurious as it will be for our children, or we must live on better terms. On my soul and conscience I have done every thing in my power to make you happy and contented as my wife I have not succeeded, God knows but if I have not, at least I can console myself with the knowledge of having done all that I could, and the firm conviction that the fault is not with me The fault has been entirely your own I do not say this to reprove or to reproach you perhaps it is your misfortune more than your fault, but with you only rests the power to make amends for the past by a change of conduct for the future If you will govern your irritable temper, and if you can consent to submit your will to mine, we may be reconciled and may be happy I firmly believe that husband and wife cannot live happily together upon any other terms, and it would be vain for us to be reunited unless upon a clear understanding of the conditions I propose, and a full determination to abide by them I have put this in plain language, and in a way perhaps calculated to wound your pride, but as I wish you to be under no delusion as to what I expect from you it is better to do so. I have made many concessions to you, you have followed your own will in almost every thing, and neither your happiness nor mine has been secured. It is for you well to consider the alternative and so decide. I do not ask you to make any concessions to my pride. I have no such feeling to consult in matters connected with you, nor any will to gratify further than our mutual happiness is concerned. I make these conditions solely because I know that we cannot be happy upon any other. *I desire nothing so much as a reconciliation with you provided it can be permanent.*"

The following is Mrs Butler's rejoinder. she has likewise omitted this from her '*Narrative*.' I may say, with truth, that my letter failed to produce any effect on her, or at least any good effect. for she rejected my proposal with anger and disdain, because obedience was a part of it.

"I have already promised to *endeavour* to control my temper, to promise more with my nervous, excitable temperament, and the temptations to irritation which naturally spring out of our differences of disposition, would be unwise and unwarrantable. My temper, or, as I must be allowed to call it, my temperament, will probably furnish me with severe moral labour, and those who love me and live with me, with exercise for their forbearance and charity, until I die. I cannot, therefore, *promise* to govern it, for that will probably be my life's lesson, in which my friends, I trust will help, not hinder me. For your second condition, that I will *submit myself to your will*, I am sorry to say that I cannot entertain this proposal for a moment. I consider it my duty *not* to submit my conduct to the government of any other human being, but could I for a moment think of giving my conscience into other hands than my own, *which is precisely the same thing*, though I love you better than any other living creature, my affection does not so far blind my judgment as to suggest you as fit for such a charge , and indeed, the few persons I know, who appear to me to be so, would conscientiously shrink from such an undue responsibility I am sorry you wrote me what you did, though when I had read but the first line, I was on the point of running to your room, for your first condition I had already promised to conform to with my most earnest endeavour and your second I had already told you, most distinctly, I never *could* accede to "

This letter, of course put an end to further attempts at reconciliation There seemed to be no remedy for such a case as hers The decided and unconquerable preference exhibited for the freedom of her own will and action, over her duty to husband and children, left me no alternative I could do nothing but leave her to the enjoyment of that uncompromising liberty, the surrender of which in her opinion had no equivalent

As I have said Mrs Butler left me at the Clarendon Hotel, and went to reside with her sister, and I went with my children to occupy the house I had taken for the residue of my stay in London While she was at her sister s, Mrs Sartoris came to see me, and urged a reconciliation I told her, as I had told Mrs Butler, that she could not be more anxious than I was to effect it, but that her sister would live with me only upon her own terms and conditions, which were peculiar to herself, and which, after a long trial, I had found impracticable I assured her that I exacted no more in the way of acquiescence and obedience than other and the best wives acknowledged and yielded to their husbands, no more, in fact, than she herself. Mrs Sartoris, yielded to her own husband She said that her sister appeared to be reasonable and willing to do all I required and that when she talked to us separately, there really seemed to be no essential difference in our views After this visit I received the following letter from Mrs Butler it is the second of the four she has published, and is marked "Exhibit B' in her "*Narrative*"

"In consequence of your refusing to be reconciled to me, or live with me, upon any but impossible terms, I came to my sister s house, in order to recover a little from the dreadful state of nervous excitement into which I had been thrown by your treatment of me and your rejection of all my attempts to restore, if not the happiness, at least the peace and tranquillity of our lives I have now recovered my composure, and having been here for several days without receiving any communication whatever from you, presume that it is your determined resolution that we should separate, and, accordingly, must now consider what my situation is likely to be, and how best to make arrangements for the future Before doing so, however let me remind you that, within the last ten days, I have made repeated and ineffectual appeals to your affection, your compassion, your justice and your humanity I have entreated your pardon for any and all my past offences, as humbly as it becomes one who has undoubtedly often been in fault to do *I now do so again*. I have offered you every assurance which a fallible human being may dare to offer of my desire and purpose of fulfilling my duty better *I now do so again*, in the hope that, tendering you all of repentance for the past and resolution for the future, that one rational creature should to another, you may be induced to reflect upon your own share in the wreck of our peace, and perhaps perceive that the further claim you have made upon me is such as your conscience should no more al-

low you to offer than mine will permit me to accept. In the event,
however, of your still adhering to this proposition which I still unequivocally refuse, it remains to make some arrangement for my future existence. My sister leaves town on Monday. I shall not
remain in her house after her departure. Perhaps as you have undertaken the management of your own household you might choose
to make such arrangements as, by enabling us to live *entirely separate,* would also restore me to my children, from whom I have in
nowise deserved to be parted whose loss is unutterably grievous to
me, and who must suffer in many ways from my absence. In pro-
posing this arrangement to you namely an entirely separate establishment, though in the same house I must explain the motives that
lead me to suggest this plan. You have apparently lost all affection
and regard for me, and have attained such a state of indifference
towards me, that you can see me meet me, and speak to me as you
would to one of your servants, or a common acquaintance while
in every essential of intimate intercourse, affection confidence, kindness we are utterly estranged, and have as little in common, whether
of sentiment or interest, as two people who had never seen each
other till yesterday. This state of things appears perfectly agreeable, or at least endurable to you, it is not so to me. I told you so
the other day, I now repeat it, together with my reasons for not being able to endure it, which I also laid before you the other day.
Having loved you well enough to give you my life, when it was best
worth giving, having made you the centre of all my hopes of earthly
happiness, having never loved any human being as I have loved you,
you can never be to me like any other human being, and it is utterly
impossible that I should ever regard you with indifference. My
whole existence having once had you for its sole object, and all its
thoughts, hopes, affections, and passions having, in their full harvest,
been yours, as you well know they were, it is utterly impossible that
I should forget this—that I should forget that you were once my lover
and are my husband, and the father of my children. Such love as

K

mine has been for you, might, in evil hearts and by evil means, be turned to hatred, but, be sure, it never can become indifference in any one, nor in me can it as certainly ever become hatred. I cannot behold you without emotion, my heart still answers to your voice, my blood in my veins to your footsteps, and if this emotion is to be one of perpetual pain sudden, violent, intense almost intolerable pain, judge how little I am endowed by nature with a temperament fit to endure so severe and incessant a trial. My intercourse with you, if not a source of happiness, becomes one of anguish, and the necessary communion which a life of intimacy brings, furnishes perpetually occasions of suffering greater than I can bear. I have told you this already, I appealed to your humanity when after a prolonged season of this species of mental torture, I found myself from a combination of moral and physical causes, so nearly deprived of my senses as to be upon the point of destroying myself. I entreated you to save me from the horrible state of nervous malady into which this very kind of intercourse with you had thrown me. God knows your answer was hardly that of a man, much less of a friend or husband. However, it is to avoid paroxysms of excitement, springing from nervous irritability, which I felt might lead me to the most fatal results, and which arise in great part from physical causes not under my own control, that I propose an entire separation from you, if you still refuse me an entire reconciliation. I dare not expose myself to influences which I have not strength to resist, and if my intercourse with you is not to be one of kindness and cordiality, I cannot attempt to make it what on my part it can never be, one of indifference and careless estrangement. My disappointment cries aloud in my heart whenever I see you, and the recollection of the past gives such bitter poignancy to the present, and such terrible gloom to the future, that my senses seem ready to forsake me, at the sight of the piteous wreck of my whole existence laid at your feet—remember with what entire faith and love. If, however, you will not consent that I should return to live under the same roof with my children upon these terms, I have but one alternative left—to hire a lodging if possible, in the same house with my father, if not, as near to him as possible, and take up my abode either with, or close to him It will be indispensably necessary that I should get a servant, as I have no human being to do anything for me and though, while in your house, I could dispense with a maid, and have done so at your desire, I cannot, alone as I now am, do without one These necessary expenses of my maintenance of course you will provide for, as you do not I presume, anticipate my becoming a burden to any of the members of my own family, nor indeed should I for a moment consent to do so This then, is the last proposal I have to make , and should I not receive an answer from you before Monday, I shall conclude that it is the one you wish me to adopt, and shall act accordingly '

This letter so full of passionate feeling, contains, nevertheless, the reservation never lost sight of and never yielded She says, " In consequence of your " refusing to be reconciled to me, or to live with me, " upon any but impossible terms, and the further " claim you have made upon me is such as your con- " science should no more allow you to offer than mine " will permit me to accept In the event however of " your still adhering to this proposition, which I still " unequivocally refuse, it remains for me to make some " arrangement for my future existence ' These ' im- possible terms," and this " further claim which she " still unequivocally refused ' were the customary and pledged acquiescence of a wife to marital control— nothing more As it is unnecessary to argue a point generally conceded, and always absurd to attempt proving an acknowledged truth, nothing is required to show the error of this principle of equal rights in marriage so obstinately contended for no one, who is not morally or intellectually astray, can fail to feel and see the heartlessness and falsity of the pretension

Her declarations on this matter of equal rights were so perversely frequent and so emphatic, that there appeared to be no hope of reconciling our differences, notwithstanding the strong mutual feeling which still existed She had established for her own peculiar use a set of intractable notions which put domestic peace at defiance, and overthrew in the household all discipline and subordination, except those of her own making and without being willing to abandon any one of these notions, she nevertheless expected me to live with her upon her own terms She had declared in language most unequivocal that she "considered it 'her duty *not* to submit her conduct to the government 'of any other human being," yet she claimed me as her husband and she emphatically added that, could she for a moment think of doing such a thing, her judgment would not be so far blinded by her affection as to suggest that this husband was fit for such a charge * In another letter she declares, "the power to pursue 'duty and right as I am able to conceive them, is of "course of more value to me than *any thing* else be-'sides † And in another, she says "I think that it 'has led me to reflect upon some passages of our inter-"course with self-condemnation, and a desire to discharge my duty to you more faithfully, than I may 'hitherto have done Yet do not now mistake me. "you ask me in your last how I like my independence,

* See page 70   † See page 87

"and whether I remember how vehemently and fre-
"quently I objected to your control over my actions —
"I remember all this well and part of my regret in con-
' templating the past, arises from the *manner* of my re-
"sistance not the fact itself Whether one person can
' or ought to exercise control over another I think is a
"question your own justice and good sense would an-
"swer at once Neither my absence from you, nor my
"earnest desire to be again with you can make me ad-
"mit that the blessed and happy relationship, in which
"we stand to each other, is any thing but perfect com-
"panionship, perfect friendship, perfect love For the
"existence of these justice must also exist, and there
"is no justice in the theory that one rational creature
"is to be subservient to another"* And in another
"letter, "It is not in the law of my conscience to pro-
"mise implicit obedience to a human being fallible like
"myself, and who can by no means relieve me of the
"responsibility of my actions before God Upon these
"grounds I could not promise obedience to any one "†
In short, nearly the whole of her married life had been
consumed in contending that she had a husband who
was not a husband—an automaton of "companionship, friendship, and love,' without any rights, and
whose endeavours to guide and rule his own family
she was at liberty to oppose and defy

I had suffered too many trials to be willing to incur the almost certain risk of again going through
what had so frequently happened, namely, a quarrel,
a separation, and a reconciliation,—and again a quarrel; and if this last appeal did not find an immediate

* See page 10   † See page 11

response on my part, it arose from the conviction that I ought not to rely, as I had too often done before, entirely on these eloquent protestations, and on love, passionate indeed, at times, but unyielding and without concession I hoped for something more reliable and I waited in the hope that some influence would lead her to perceive her error and that our next reconciliation, which I longed for no less earnestly than herself, might be more enduring, when it did happen, than our former ones

In naming the conditions in her letter upon which she was willing to live with her family, she proposes first, to live with me upon her own terms—mine she "unequivocally refuses ' second, if her terms do not suit me—she proposes "to live entirely separate," and to have ' an entirely separate establishment, though in the same house " and her third and last proposal—in case I will not consent to either of her others—is, " to hire a lodging, if possible, in the same " house with her father, if not, as near him as possible, ' and take up her abode either with, or close to him " And she adds, this then is the last proposal I have "to make, and should I not receive an answer from " you before Monday, I shall conclude that it is the one "you wish me to adopt, and shall act accordingly." She did not wait, however, to receive an answer from me to her various suggestions but, deciding the question for herself, came to live in my house the very day after she wrote me this letter Her return to her family was in this wise I had lived in this new abode for about a week, during which time Mrs Butler lived with her sister, when late one night, just at twelve o'clock, there was a loud knocking at the front door,

the servants were all in bed I was the only person
up, and I answered the summons to the door myself
it was Mrs Butler come back again

I must not omit to mention that during this week
she came once each day to see the children and remained with them about half an hour , but as she had
not given me the least intimation of an intention to
return to her family, except upon the terms named in
her letter, which as yet I had not replied to, her visit
at such an unusual hour was entirely unlooked for, no
arrangements had been made for her coming, and the
servants had to be called out of bed to prepare a room
for her

After this midnight return, we continued to live in
the same house but for some time entirely separate,
even at our meals and maintaining distinct establish-
ments, which the size of the house enabled me to do
When we received invitations to the houses of our
friends, our answers were returned separately, and,
when accepted, we did not go together This was
soon remarked, it gave painful concern to our friends
led them to a knowledge of the way in which we
lived, and finally brought about their interposition

It may be asked, if on these occasions I never appealed to Mr Kemble to exercise some influence over
his daughter, and to endeavour to set her right? I
did not Mr Kemble is a man of mild and gentle
disposition, and in no way calculated to control the
very opposite nature of his daughter Moreover,
I knew he would be very unwilling to interfere between us, and consequently never referred our difficulties to him

Those friends who did interpose proved themselves

kind, judicious, and what is above all, just   The very
reverse of some of the persons into whose hands Mrs
Butler has unfortunately fallen in this country   The
former laboured to effect a reconciliation. and they
succeeded   The latter may be warm partisans, but
they scarcely can be considered discreet counsellors
Could she have had the advice in October, 1843, in
Philadelphia, of those who counselled her in London,
her conduct at that time, and subsequently, would
doubtless have been widely different from what it has
been

The following letter. being ' Exhibit D," in Mrs
Butler s ' *Narrative*," was written in consequence of
urgent representations made to her by one of our
mutual friends, after several ineffectual interviews
with each of us

" You have so repeatedly and harshly repelled all my attempts to
be reconciled to you, that nothing but an imperative sense of duty
would give me courage to address you again   But our mutual friend,
Mary Mackintosh, to whom I suppose you have expressed your
state of feeling with regard to me, has earnestly urged me to make
another appeal to you, and assured me that she thought our present
estrangement was a source of as much pain to you as to me   As
you had declared both that you preferred our present mode of living
to a more friendly one, and that, moreover, in this state of separation from me you were better able to fulfil your various duties, I had
naturally felt that it could not be desirable for you to be reconciled to
me, and that after such a declaration on your part, any further attempt on mine to alter your determination was really a selfish indulgence of my own earnest wishes   If, however, Mary Mackintosh
has understood you rightly, and has represented correctly to me your
feelings, you are not happy and satisfied in our present mode of liv-

ing any more than myself, and the duty of again attempting to regain a better and less miserable condition for both of us, forces itself upon my mind I hardly know now what it is that you require of me in order to be reconciled to me When, during your indisposition, I asked you on my knees what promise it was that you exacted from me, you replied, that you desired none, and, again, last night Mary Mackintosh assured me that you had told her that *compliance* was all that you expected from me Compliance with your wishes, and obedience to your will, in every respect in which they do not interfere with the dictates of my conscience I am most ready and willing to promise you I have already expressed my extreme sorrow for all my faults, both of omission and commission towards you and my sincere determination to endevour not again either to offend or pain you If, therefore, my promise of compliance and obedience, in all things where my conscience does not forbid them may satisfy you, pray accept it, and let me again earnestly entreat you to restore your affection to me, and again to treat me as in heart and soul I have never ceased to be, your true and devoted friend, and loving wife If this letter fails of its object at any rate let me beg you to consider that I have been moved to write it, by the representations of your friend, who seemed to think that both my love and my duty imperatively required that I should again express my feelings to you, and endeavour to obtain the answer which she represented yours as likely to return "

This letter is another of those given in the *Narrative,*" as if never answered and of which she says, they "failed to produce any effect The deception involved in this assertion, and the utter disregard of fairness which the proceeding displayed will be conclusively proved by the insertion of the following reply, which most luckily for my own vindication, I am able to copy from the original corrected draft accidentally preserved, as before stated without the least idea of any use ever being made of it. The letter shall speak for itself —

" As I did not separate from you for slight causes, nor without full consideration I do not think it advisable to rush into a reconciliation, or without a clear understanding of the terms on which we are to live together in future. Having tried for some years to live according to your ideas of equal rights and mutual independence, and as we usually passed our lives in wrangling, unquietness, and contention, I slowly came to the conviction after long trials of patience and forbearance, that to live together any longer upon such terms was neither desirable nor possible, and that unless a great alteration took place in your conduct, I would live apart from you, leaving you to the free indulgence of your own most determined will. Trusting, however, to the strength of your affection and to your earnestly expressed desire for a reconciliation, I yielded to my own feelings and to your wishes, and agreed to make another trial of living together, without having received a promise of that obedience, which I am convinced it is your duty to yield. I did so, in the hope and trust that the experience, and time for reflection, you had had, would convince you of the necessity of acting with more compliance towards me than you had ever done before. It did not require long to prove to me that my reliance was hopeless, and that I could expect nothing but disappointment. Our daily life was soon subject to the same causes of irritation and wretchedness that had usually beset it. This confirmed me in the opinion I had always held, but which I had forborne to enforce, that without obedience from a wife to her husband, it is utterly impossible to live happily together. The natural disposition of most women, which is gentle and yielding, leads them to act with a spirit of compliance towards their husbands, and to consult their wishes in most things. In such cases there is no claim of obedience, it is not needed, compliance is willingly and freely yielded, and nothing more is desired. Nor do I desire any thing more, if I could but obtain that. Unfortunately your natural disposition so frequently prompts you to act in direct opposition to all my wishes and desires, and with hostility to my interests and your extraordinary strength of will makes you for the time so inaccessible to entreaty, persuasion, or to reason, that I am forced to claim my right and the fulfilment of your duty and to exact that obedience which a different spirit on your part would render unnecessary. You have always refused to acknowledge that obedience was any part of your duty as a wife and have maintained that a wife has the same right to follow her own wishes to act upon her own opinion, and to indulge her own whims and fancies as freely and as fully as her husband and you have not failed to act up to your principles on that point so that I have had neither obedience nor compliance from you. My past experience would not lead me to expect much of the latter, but obedience you may at all times yield, if you but choose to do so. Your letter contains the first intimation you have ever given me of any disposition or willingness to yield obedience, heretofore you have always said, I will promise no obedience, do not expect it.' You now tell me, that compliance with my wishes, and obedience to my will in every respect in which they do not interfere with the dictates of your conscience you are most ready and willing to promise me. This is the engagement that every woman enters into when she marries—it does not signify what ceremony of marriage is used—and it is the fulfilment of this obligation, voluntarily and solemnly entered into by you, that I require. I do not propose any new or unusual condition. The promise that you now offer is indeed all that I require but until now you have ever refused to make any such promise. If, therefore, you solemnly and deliberately and with a firm determination to keep it do make me this promise, there is no bar to our reconciliation. But as I do not wish you to deceive yourself nor to be again disappointed myself I wish to have the clearest understanding between us, and I fairly tell you that I shall expect and exact your promise to its entire extent So long as you continue to act in a spirit of compliance—as you did for a short time after our reconciliation at Liverpool—there will be no occasion for me to claim obedience, but there are times when you are possessed with a determined spirit of resistance to every body and to every thing, but more particularly towards me and my wishes, these have so continually occurred that I fear they will recur again, and then you will not act with compliance, and it will be necessary for me to claim that obedience, which you are now willing to promise me. Before you confirm that promise, I desire you to think well of it I have twice separated myself from you, and I have been once reconciled to you upon your own terms, relying upon the assurances of affection and compliance which you gave me These soon failed, and again I was obliged to leave you to the enjoyment of your will, for you would do nothing that I wished I then found that without obedience on your part we could not live together, and until you would make such a promise, I would not again attempt it It is because I wish our reconciliation to be permanent, that I ask you to think well of your promise, which I may have occasion to claim to its fullest extent I have separated from you on principle, and from necessity, not from temper, and if we are now reconciled to each other, and you again oblige me to leave you, it will be for the last time It is necessary also to have a clear understanding as to the reservation which you make with regard to your conscience You promise obedience to my will in every respect in which it does not interfere with the dictates of your conscience You have often confounded will with conscience and may do so again, and when you are strongly bent on doing any thing you may fancy that the dictates of your conscience impel you to do it My claim of obedience does not go to the extent of expecting a wife to do what is positively wrong, or sinful, at her husband's bidding, she would be justified in refusing any such demand, and every one would support her in it But fortunately right and wrong are not matters of opinion, those points have been settled for us, and to distinguish between them is one of the characteristics of a sane mind. It is not very probable, therefore, that I shall ever demand of you to do what is unfit, or wrong, but in case you should ever imagine that the dictates of your conscience oblige you to do what is opposed to my wishes I do expect that you will not act hastily, or from sudden impulse, but that you will take time calmly to deliberate upon it, and that you will also consult those friends in whom you have confidence, and if they do not support you in your opinion, that the point in disagreement between us does involve conscience, that then you will refrain from acting against my wishes. If you can make up your mind to this, then we may be reconciled, and if you will act towards me with a spirit of compliance, there will be no need for my claiming your promise of obedience, and I doubt not, but that we may live most happily together "

The following is Mrs Butler's reply she has altogether omitted this also from her '*Narrative*'

" There is but one part of the long letter I received from you this morning, which requires an answer, and I therefore confine myself to that, leaving without comment the various positions and assertions contained in the rest of it. The conclusion, containing the specific statement of what you expect from me, is the only portion of it to which I suppose you look for a reply. You say that (in the event of your being reconciled to me), should any case arise between us, in which I imagine that the dictates of my conscience oblige me to do what is opposed to your wishes, you expect that I will not act hastily and from sudden impulse, but that I will take time calmly to deliberate upon it. To this I am very ready to agree, and shall think myself benefitted by any promise, which may assist me to postpone the decisions of my feelings to those of my judgment. Further you say, that in such case you will also expect me to consult those friends in whom I have confidence, and if they do not support me in my opinion, that the point in disagreement between us does involve conscience, that I will then refrain from acting against your wishes With the first part of this demand I am very willing to promise compliance, namely, that in any case in which my own sense of right runs counter to your wishes, I should consult the friends in whose wisdom and excellence I have faith, and allow their opinions the full weight they deserve in modifying mine, but I cannot possibly promise to abide by their decision, should it, after calm and mature deliberation be contrary to my own positive conviction of what is right This transfer of my own conscience, whether to one or several individuals, is a thing which I consider sinful in the highest degree, and which of course I cannot promise Due deliberation in the exercise of my own judgment, and a patient reference to the judgment of others, I am perfectly ready to promise, but the last tribunal, the supreme one, and from which there should be no appeal, is conscience—the conscience of the individual him or herself—God's spirit, which he has himself ordained as paramount, and to promise to place this in the hands of others is what I dare not do You must judge for yourself, whether the compliance I offer with your conditions is likely to satisfy you I have desired our reunion most ardently, but there are certain prices at which nothing is to be purchased and the surrender of conscience is a sinful sacrifice which has no equivalent '

This subject of ' conscience" is dwelt on so much, and adhered to so obstinately by Mrs Butler, that it might very well lead any one to infer that she was frequently in danger of being required to do violence to it or that there were times when she was called upon in some way to disobey some direct command of God So far from this being the case, no question ever arose between us which by any possibility could be supposed to involve "conscience," unless it be that of negro slavery The position that she assumed on this topic was not a strong one indeed, it scarcely could be considered as tenable at all The act of marrying a slave owner, made her also a slave owner, and her support as well as mine was derived from the product of slave labour Nor did her idea of duty, or "conscience ' ever impel her openly to take up arms against this alleged evil, except on two occasions, when she was solicited to do so by editors of abolition publications, who sought her aid to promote their own views Then, and only then did she insist upon bearing her testimony publicly against slavery so that in fact her ' conscience ' was moved to the point of thus expressing her views, only when stirred to it by the suggestion or the request of others , and then indeed it became so imperative on her, that my feelings and all my entreaties were disregarded

Nor can the view she takes of ' duty' and ' conscience' be considered as entirely sound In a letter written some time before the one above she says, ' My "children s happiness does not go before *all* other "things with me, though it goes far before any con-"sideration of my own My sense of duty is to me "the vital part of life , and the freedom of my con-"science—the power to pursue duty and right as I "am able to conceive them—is of course of more value "to me than *any thing* else besides And in the foregoing letter she maintains that 'the last tribu-"nal, the supreme one, and from which there should "be no appeal, is conscience—the conscience of the "individual him or herself' The dangerous sophistry of such sentiments held by an individual, and that individual a woman, is apparent if every person be justified in exercising "the power to pursue duty and right," as he or she only is "able to conceive them," what mischief and what fatal errors would not be the necessary consequences? Before we could claim so bold and important a prerogative, we must first establish that we have an exemption from all human frailties and all false notions on matters of conduct, that we have had and used the best means of improvement to gain a perfect knowledge of our duty, and that our judgment in morals admits of no perversion and no mistake

Nor is the error of her other sentiment less apparent, namely, that the "conscience of the individual, him or herself," is "the supreme tribunal from which there should be no appeal ' This is confounding the "conscience" of the individual with the word of God, whose direct commands are alone supreme, and from which there is no appeal Duty is taught us by the cultivation of our moral perceptions, and "conscience' is the result of that intellectual discernment which enables us to distinguish right from wrong, but neither the lights nor the dictates are always so clear and so strong as to point unerringly the path to follow The moral perceptions may easily be clouded by passion, and the conscience become hardened by pride, by interest, or by prejudice It is rather rash, if not foolhardy, for any one to boast a perfectly enlightened conscience, and if we disdain the advice of others, if we do not sometimes consent "to place our conscience in the hands of others" on whose wisdom and virtue we can rely, we may do very bad things There certainly are occasions when our own internal monitor is all sufficient, these are, when we feel in-

clined to disobey some direct command of God then
conscience warns us but it is our knowledge of His
law which enlightens and guides us To suppose that
the feeling which we call conscience ' will if obeyed,
always guide us clear of error, is the common and
pernicious fallacy of a self-righteous spirit to yield implicitly to either its silence or its suggestions would
enlarge our self-reliance to such an extent as to make
that quality a dangerous possession, and no one, who
earnestly seeks to do right will follow exclusively the
light of his own mind, or venture to rely in all cases
on his own ideas of duty

One of the most marked features in Mrs Butler s
character is an entire self-reliance in matters of opinion, it is so unmeasured as to produce a conviction
of her own infallibility it causes her to adhere obstinately to her own views on every subject, and it
has led her into much of the error of her life

As her last letter brought us somewhat nearer to
the point that we both appeared desirous to reach
and as it was useless, if not absurd to contend longer
about this point of ' conscience," I sought an interview with Mrs Butler, hoping to effect more by conversation than by again writing This interview did
not result, however, so satisfactorily as I had been
led to hope, and we parted without accomplishing a
reconciliation Soon after I received the following
letter from her —this, and my reply to it have also
been omitted from her " *Narrative* '

" I do not know whether you had any intention or desire of being
reconciled to me just now It has occurred to me since you left me,

M

that perhaps you had, and that some concession on my part would have induced you to do so As I am aware that it is my duty to endeavour by all means to be reconciled to you if possible, I am willing to make every exertion for that purpose

' You seemed to expect some promise from me with regard to the future, but those who have failed as signally as I have done in the past, can surely hardly dare to *promise* for the future One thing, however I can promise, which is to *endeavour heartily* to do my duty better henceforward than I have done it hitherto More than this, I dare not say, for I know myself most fallible, and can hardly hope to escape temptation, if this can satisfy you, pray accept it. I am most unwilling that pride, or any other evil thing should prevent my using every endeavour to conciliate you, and I am aware that I have been so often in fault towards you, that though I may not have much hope for the future, I have much regret for the past "

I could ask nothing more than this it was all I had ever desired or expected, and more than she had ever offered before I returned the following brief reply —

' I am quite satisfied with the promises you have made me, and if you will adhere to them—to the spirit of them rather than to the letter—our reunion will be happy and lasting "

Our reconciliation took place immediately and we again lived together on happy terms, for her promises were kept both in the spirit of them and to the letter

This better state of things between us was brought about in the month of February, 1843, and we continued to live together on good terms after this, maintaining every relation of husband and wife, for the remainder of our stay in England, while we crossed the

Atlantic, and for a short time after our return to the United States, which was in May, 1843

Mrs Butler's 'Narrative' contains the following statement —

"From the autumn of 1842, although under the same roof we lived separate and with a general discontinuance of all the intercourse of husband and wife, and his treatment of me was such for a length of time habitually that I should have been warranted by the law of God and the land to depart wholly from his house, and never see him more without incurring the charge of desertion or any other breach of my duty'

This statement, as will be seen from what has gone before it, is simply untrue

One of the four letters referred to namely, Exhibit C" in the 'Narrative' has not been given above it is inserted here

' I hear with great pain that you are ill I dare not come to you for fear of annoying and irritating you, but I implore you to let me come to you and be with you while you are suffering and helpless Oh, Pierce, I love you dearly, pray let me come and nurse you, and do anything in the world I can for you I am miserable to hear of your illness, only send me word that I may come—pray pray, do, dear Pierce "

The original of this, which is now before me, was written apparently in haste, on a little blotted scrap of paper it was a missive from one room to another in the same house, just before our reconciliation took place it seemed like the irrepressible outpouring of affectionate feeling and as such it was received by me

When these four letters appeared in print it struck many as very singular that copies of them even to this little outpouring, had been taken and retained, and I have been asked more than once ' are you "sure you have the originals ? May she not have got "them back again?" These originals are before me they have never left my possession since they were received, and it could only be from copies carefully made at the time each was written, that they have been printed in the " *Narrative* "

DISUNION

AFTER our return to Philadelphia, in May, 1843, Mrs Butler's conduct which since our reconciliation in London had enabled us to live together on comfortable terms, soon relapsed into its old waywardness and irregularity She totally disregarded what she had promised at the time of our reconciliation in England —" Compliance with your wishes, and obedience " to your will, in every respect in which they do not " interfere with the dictates of my conscience, I am " most ready and willing to promise you ' * She exhibited now, as formerly, strange perverseness of action and determined opposition to my wishes One instance, out of many, will suffice I went in the summer of that year, 1843, to the Chester Springs, or, as they are more commonly called, the Yellow Springs, about thirty miles from Philadelphia, intending to pass the hot weather there At this place is a large natural spring-bath the hours for using it are, with ladies, before twelve o clock with gentlemen, from twelve until two o'clock, the last being the hour for dining My family was here for several weeks, I usually

* See page 81

passed Saturday and Sunday with them, the other days of the week I was in the city. Once, on going to the Springs as usual, I was informed by the nurse of my children, that she and they had been subjected to an unpleasant occurrence in consequence of Mrs Butler's having taken them into the bath at the time appropriated exclusively to gentlemen. I gave her strict orders not, on any account, to remain there after twelve o'clock. I also told Mrs Butler that the rules of the establishment must be observed, and that she must conform to the appointed hours. At the end of another week I again learned that Mrs Butler had continued to infringe the gentlemen's hour for bathing, that her doing so had given rise to much dissatisfaction and complaint, and that she would probably bring something unpleasant upon herself, for the Springs had become quite crowded, and the time assigned to gentlemen was scarcely sufficient to accommodate them all. I now told her that if she persisted in such conduct I must leave the Springs, as I feared she would provoke insult and involve me in personal altercation. She paid no manner of regard to what I said. It was Sunday, as the last ladies were quitting the bathing-room she took possession of it by herself, and remained in it until long past twelve o'clock, while a crowd of gentlemen were impatiently waiting, by no means in the best temper at this encroachment upon their privilege. My only alternative was to leave the place, I did so, the same afternoon, and returned most unwillingly to the hot city with my children in the middle of the month of August.

Choosing to have the confirmation of others in regard to her conduct in this instance, I have obtained a letter from Mr Holman, the manager of the establishment, which is here inserted, together with the letter I wrote to him on the subject —

' *Philadelphia, January* 14, 1850

" Dear Sir,

" If the suit instituted by me for a divorce had been tried, as at one time I fully expected, you would have received a subpœna and been summoned as a witness in the case. You would have been examined as to Mrs Butler's conduct, and the effect of it during my visit to the Yellow Springs in the summer of 1843, while your mother was proprietor of the place, and you had the direction of the hotel

' You will oblige me by stating now, in writing, exactly what you would have said, if you had been put under oath on the witness stand

" Yours, &c

" PIERCE BUTLER

" SAM HOLMAN,

" *Yellow Springs, Chester County, Pa*

' *Chester Springs, January* 16, 1850.

" Dear Sir,

" Your letter of the 14th instant was duly received, asking me to state in writing, what Mrs Butler's conduct was in regard to her infringing the rules at our bathing establishment, during her sojourn with us in the summer of 1843 In answer I would state that our rules for bathing, as painted and hung over the bath door, were, ' Ladies' hours from 10 to 12 o'clock Gentlemen's, before 10 and after 12 ' Information was given to me at the bar, that Mrs Butler had occupied the bath at different times long after the hours allotted for ladies to bathe, and as our dinner hour was 2 o'clock gentlemen could not get into the bath before dinner, and if she persisted in so doing they would be under the necessity of forcing the door upon her There was considerable company at the Springs at the time, and the dissatisfaction was pretty general among the gentlemen. the door was not forced, as you arrived at the Springs soon after, and took your family off This is the substance of all I know

"I am, very respectfully,

' Your obedient servant,

"Sam Holman

"Pierce Butler, Esq , *Philadelphia* "

This state of obstinate opposition, thwarting all I asked and had a right to expect, grew worse and worse, her constant tone of mind towards me was that of mingled resentment and defiance, and her temper seemed incapable of abatement or repose Still I had courage and patience to bear up in these ceaseless trials while there was any hope of her abiding with her children, but now all good influences appeared to leave her, and she became more firmly determined than ever to carry out her long meditated plan of separation She consulted a legal adviser, Mr Gerhard, who called to his assistance Mr Meredith If she had consulted only these two gentlemen, it would perhaps have been better for her, or, as I have before remarked, had her friends and advisers here proved as judicious and just as those who counselled her in England, her course at this crisis would probably have been very different But unfortunately she fell into bad hands, she poured out her complaints to persons who only fanned the fire of her temper, who exasperated rather than soothed her, and who by their odious and pernicious intermeddling helped to complete the wreck of my happiness

She now finally withdrew herself from all intercourse with me communicating her determination to
do so in the following characteristic note —

"In consequence of your infidelity towards me and your ill treatment of me I have come to the determination to be separated from
you I have consulted Mr Gerhard upon the subject and must refer you to him as my counsel *in which capacity* is he has declined
visiting me here (since I have consulted him professionally), without
your knowledge and consent. I wish to know if you have any objection to my receiving him here

⋅Fanny

"*Friday, 27th October,*" [1843]

I returned no answer to this note, and received a
visit in relation to it from Mr Theodore Sedgwick
He came to my chamber where at the time I was confined to my bed by illness Mrs Butler he said, desired a reply to her inquiry as her counsel declined
calling upon her until assured that I did not object to
his doing so I told Mr Sedgwick that she was at
liberty to receive her counsel but I would hold no
communication with that counsel as such, nor would
I be a party to any formal contract of separation
At the same time I expressed my perfect willingness
to talk to him Mr Sedgwick about my affairs as he
stood in the light of a mutual friend He wished me,
he said, so to consider him and distinctly represented
himself, not as Mrs Butler's legal assistant, but as a
friend to both parties with the sole desire of doing
good to both Mrs Butler's present aversion to me,
I then said, seemed so bitter, and her intention of separating from me so fixed, that I should put no obsta-

cle in her way, nor did I wish her to live with me in violence to her feelings, but, I added, no necessity whatever existed for the interference of lawyers, as I would make an arrangement to secure her a perfectly independent residence, such as she desired, and that he, our mutual friend, should communicate its details to her   I offered two thousand five hundred dollars a year for her support, and as we were then at lodgings she could have apartments distinct from mine, though under the same roof, and thus be able to maintain a constant intercourse with her children, with which I should not interfere   nor indeed should I interfere with her in any way   while she conformed to three conditions deemed by me indispensable, namely, not to go on the stage—not to advocate in print the abolition cause—and not to publish any writings disapproved by me —as either of these three acts would annul the arrangement

Some days subsequently I received the following from Mr Sedgwick —

"*New York, November* 6, 1843.

" My dear Butler,

" In our conversation on Sunday before last you stated to me that you would not be a party to any formal separation with Mrs Butler But that if she determined to live apart from you, you would interpose no obstacle to her so doing   That you would pay her monthly or quarterly for her separate use one-third of your income, not to be less for the present (and until you had ascertained exactly the amount of your income) than twenty-five hundred dollars, that she might reside either at the same place you reside in or in another that she preferred, and that she might have free intercourse with her children as often and as constantly as she pleased, as much so in short as at present The only terms you attached to this offer were that she was not to go on the stage not to publish anything of which you disapproved, and not to avow herself an abolitionist, that either of these things would alone put an end to all intercourse with the children and all dependence on you

'In the event of this being handed to you Mrs Butler will have determined to accept the proposition and I have then to say that she desires the payments to be made to me, that I will receive them, and that she wishes the first monthly or quarterly payment to be made at once, and hereafter in advance, as this I suppose must be a matter of indifference to you

           "I am very truly yours

                "THEODORE SEDGWICK

"PIERCE BUTLER, Esq, *Philadelphia*"

The following was my reply —

               '*Philadelphia, Nov.* 8, 1843

"My dear Sedgwick,

"Your letter dated the 6th instant has been handed to me, and as you advise me, I receive it as a formal and deliberate declaration on the part of my wife that it is her wish and intention to live apart from me, to be separated from me

"As I do not desire her to live with me against her inclination, I shall offer no opposition to her resolution You recapitulate the subject of a conversation between us on Sunday, 29th of October last. It is correct except in one particular, and in that you have misapprehended me, 'That she might reside either at the same place you reside in, or in any other that she preferred, and that she might have free intercourse with her children as often and as constantly as she pleased, as much so in short as at present' It must be obvious to you that this could not be so, after she withdraws herself from my family, and ceases to be a member of it Her wish for a separation seems to be deliberate, and her determination fixed, and therefore I no longer consider her as forming part of my family. I should not prevent the children from going to see her, nor should I object to her coming into my house to see them, but how can she 'reside at the same place I reside in,' and be separated from me?

"I said that she could live in this house, or in any other that she preferred' but it is plain that she could not live in my house, nor could she continue to exercise any domestic control, after resolving of her own free will to be separated from me. This house is public, and it is only in my own apartments that I have control, she can, no doubt, engage other apartments here, and so live here if she like, but when I go into a house of my own my arrangements will be made without any reference to her, and I shall take the entire direction of my family, as I was obliged to do at one time in England, when she left my house. I have no wish to prescribe any course to her, but I must know distinctly her intention.

"I offered one-third of my income for her separate use but of course that was meant for her entire support. She could not expect to receive this proportion and live at the same time in my house. If she wishes to do so, or to live in my apartments while here, a sum shall be set apart for her separate use but it must necessarily be less than one-third, as it would be for personal expenses only. There is no difficulty as regards the amount if it be for her support, one-third shall be paid regularly.

"In the mean time, and until this is settled, I shall allow her the exclusive use of one of the rooms, presuming that she will withdraw to her own apartments on receiving the first payment on account of one-third of my income per year.

"Yours, very sincerely,

"PIERCE BUTLER"

It is with reluctance that I introduce the names of other persons into this statement, but the share they

voluntarily took in my domestic troubles renders it unavoidable At this unhappy period no less than four members of the Sedgwick family hastened to Philadelphia, officiously and offensively to intermeddle with my private concerns, and their conduct formed so strong a contrast to what it always had been at prior periods, that I am forced to speak of it without reserve Their professions of friendship, and my unabated reliance on them up to this time, render their subsequent change and treachery towards me the more glaring and I think their behaviour justifies all I say of them They received Mrs Butler's exaggerations without question, they sought no disavowal or explanation from me nor did they venture to seem for a moment to doubt the truth of her accusations Intimately acquainted with the peculiarities of her disposition, they had long since ascertained the danger they would incur by differing from one so "morbidly susceptible to reproof or disapprobation '*
Years before they had depicted her traits correctly, and subsequent intercourse had rendered their knowledge of her singular and impracticable nature more exact and correct Mrs Sedgwick had assured her that 'her mind was positively and greatly diseased. "and that she had herself been the cause of all that appearance of indifference in her husband which "she now believed to be the original source of her "unhappiness † She had also said to her, "My "dearest Fanny, believe me, you are altogether mor- "bid on this subject You have the best means of "happiness that this world ever furnishes, in your

"power and still you are wretched You have af-
"fluence, a husband whose love you do not ques-
"tion as fine children as mortal was ever blessed
"with, and rare gifts of mind and heart, but you
"inherit undoubtedly, from your mother, those mor-
"bid tendencies which poison and spoil all ' "Did
"you not tell me once, that you admired Kate's dis-
"cernment in telling you that she did not believe you
"could be very happy in any situation ' And surely,
"surely you will find it so " "I assure you there
"are those things in every married woman's life,
"which, if she were constituted as you are, would
"make her as wretched as you " "But, my dearest
"Fanny, even if you still persist in your belief, that
"you are a wronged and injured woman although
"your convictions may remain just the same, in spite
"of all I can say, still I do not think that they afford
"the slightest justification for your leaving your hus-
"band " "You voluntarily put yourself in the way
"of becoming a mother, and I cannot think of a more
"heinous offence against God and right, than to cast
"off this duty ' "You have an immense trust re-
"posed in you, think what it is to have such a soul
"as Sarah's put into your keeping, and will you con-
"sign it to any chance care? Will you throw it away
"from you, as a vexed child tosses away her play
"thing?' "My poor, dear Fanny, my precious, al-
"most idolized friend, do let me persuade you, that
"your mind is diseased How can you do this great
"iniquity and sin against God? If, indeed, a mind in
"such a state as yours is morally responsible You
"have, dear, great confidence in me, in my sense of
"right, so much, that I have sometimes wondered

"how I came to inspire it, but since it is so, do put
"yourself under my guidance for a little time, do not
"act rashly, or hastily"*

But experience had taught them that such honest,
wholesome admonition was not the way to keep on
good terms with Mrs Butler, it was not palatable,
she took it impatiently, it irritated, and there was
danger of her quarrelling also with them they knew
full well that no advice would be acceptable which did
not sanction and stimulate her animosity towards myself to offer counsel at variance with her excited
feelings, would be construed into want of sympathy,
the ardour of their friendship would be suspected and
they incurred the imminent risk of being regarded
as lukewarm if not something worse They knew
that to prolong their intimacy with one they must
wholly abandon the other, and they had no hesitation
in doing so, at a time, too, when their cooler and
firmer judgment might really have been of service to
both

One of the four members of this family, who, as I
have said, came to Philadelphia at this crisis to mix
themselves up in my domestic disquietudes, was Mrs
Charles Sedgwick She came uninvited I received
her, however, as usual But I soon found her manner towards me changed and after she had been with
us a day or two, I received from her the following
extraordinary letter —

"*Sunday, A M Nov* 5, 1843

'You have been kind to me, and I have been a true friend to you,
but you must be aware that we stand no longer upon the same foot-

* Mrs Sedgwick s letter, pp 41, 42, 43

ing as formerly, that I regard you as having deliberately and deeply injured the dearest friend that I have upon earth out of my own family, and that my sympathy with her is that of a woman, as well as of a friend You must recollect your having told me the last spring that you had never sinned against Fanny in any way The declaration appeared to me at the time to imply an incredible degree of self-delusion what must I think of it now? Can I respect your truth or sin against my own, by appearing to regard you as formerly? I have no feeling of unkindness towards you, nothing to prevent my exchanging the common salutations of civility with you, nothing to prevent my praying God, as I have already done many times, to bring you back to him, but there can no longer be friendship, or even the appearance of it, between us Under these circumstances I am aware that I ought not without permission to seat myself at the same meals with you, and if you prefer that I should not do so, you must tell me this, and I will go to the public table *

' E B S "

When I received this strange and impudent communication, I perceived that Mrs Sedgwick had caught the infection from the " diseased mind" of her " almost idolized friend,' but I immediately wrote the following reply —

" Nov 5, 1843.

" As my kind feelings towards you are not changed, you are as welcome at my table now as you were ever welcome in my house, when I had one to receive you in You will always be welcome when you choose to come where I am That your sympathy should be strong for your friend is but natural and though it turns you

---

* I was living at a lodging-house, in Philadelphia, where I had private apartments, and a private table Mrs Sedgwick continued to occupy my apartments, and to sit at my table, while her visit lasted

against me, it cannot mislead me so far as to alter the smallest feeling of regard that I ever felt for you Misguided herself, she has misled you Without sense, discretion or judgment to direct and control an impetuous disposition an unquiet temper, and a never satisfied mind, she rushes into errors which time can never repair, gives way to feelings of temporary animosity against me, and believing herself to be an unhappy woman, she strongly engages the sympathy of her friends for wrongs which are imaginary, and for injuries which are self-inflicted This state of feeling soon changes, and her mind for a time becomes better regulated, but the impression, that in her moments of phrensy, she has given others, unfortunately remains It is thus she injures both herself and me God, who has withheld reason from her, alone can endow her with it now, and without his aid she must walk in error as she has ever done To you, perhaps, the truth will one day appear, you will know her better than you do at present, your affection for her will not always blind you as it does now, and when you rightly perceive her failings, and her unhappy weaknesses your sympathy may be of more service to her than it can be now, when, like herself, you are under the influence of feelings engendered in error, and which for the time obscure the reason. Be sure you will one day think very differently, and when that day dawns upon you, you may rely upon my regard for you being unchanged For the monstrous wrong she does me, I freely forgive her It can never create one feeling of anger or hatred against her I think of her with the deepest commisseration, and weep,—oh! how I weep when she knows it not—that a heart so warm and true as hers, should be warped by a head so weak

"My way is before me, towards her, and towards our children, my duty shall be fulfilled God has of late endowed me with a strength that I never have felt before I feel conscious of being able to go through with my allotted task, and it shall be done

"Though faults of temper, errors of judgment, and misguided reason may estrange her feelings from me for a time, our hearts can never be disunited she knows mine too well, and as well do I know hers. Both are true If in this life the head shall continue to over-sway the heart, then must we look to the everlasting hereafter—there rightly to feel, and rightly to know each other

" You have told me that there can no longer be friendship, or even the appearance of it, between us This then may be the last com-munication that will pass between us, and I wish to tell you that your three kind letters to me last summer were received as kindly as they were written, and although I did not reply to them, I was not the less thankful and grateful I wished to accept your invita-tion to send the children to see you, but I had strong reasons for keeping them here, and regretted that I could not do as you asked. It has troubled me much lest you should think I was cold or indif-ferent to your kindness, and I will not let this opportunity pass with-out assuring you it was not so

" Pierce Butler "

In Mrs Butler's note of October 27,* in which she announces her " determination to be separated from me, ' she says, that it is in consequence of my " infi-" delity towards her, and my ill treatment of her " And Mrs Sedgwick says, that ' she regards me as " having deliberately and deeply injured the dearest " friend she has upon earth out of her family " This refers to the charge of ' infidelity, which was then, for the first time, employed against me, and was then and has ever since been made the chief groundwork on which an excuse was raised to justify Mrs Butler s separating herself from me It will scarcely be be-lieved that this imputation by Mrs Butler and her echoes was the offspring of suspicion only, and that after many exertions some silly and some disreputable, to sustain it by something in the shape of evidence, they so utterly failed as to feel the necessity of formally abandoning it Such are however the facts Mrs Butler asserted positively to her friends that I had been unfaithful and they, believing her, repeated the allegation, as the most simple and convenient mode of justifying their own conduct towards me it went forth, and was received as such scandal usually is, without proof, and defying contradiction   At that very time, when she and the Sedgwicks were circulating the accusation with the utmost positiveness, they were perfectly conscious that they were without evidence, and that it rested exclusively upon angry invectives and suspicions   But as they wished them to be true, they probably believed their surmises, and supposed it would be possible to ferret out proof of them the more so as there were not wanting persons who, to ingratiate themselves with Mrs Butler, promised to procure the desired evidence   The first attempt of this sort which came to my knowledge was made by endeavouring to enlist against me one of my domestic servants the nurse of my children   She was visited in the nursery one morning by Mrs Charles Sedgwick who dexterously strove to lead her into talking injuriously of me and to commit her into saying that my life in London had been dissipated, and that I had ill treated my wife, all of which being fresh news to the nurse, she could neither confirm, nor converse about   Failing in that she asked the nurse if I had never made any sort of an attempt upon her own virtue, which so enraged the woman, that giving her inquisitor an indignant rebuff, she immediately came to inform me of this dirty course of conduct

So despicable an intrigue, by a person sitting daily at my table, breaking the same bread with me and my children, opened my eyes to her real character, and I confessed the truth of what she had written to me, that there "could no longer be friendship, or even the appearance of it," between us two

Detected and exposed in this unworthy attempt to injure me, the malignity of a vulgar nature was awakened, and thenceforward revelled in active and bitter enmity

So frankly and implicitly had I trusted the different members of this family, that the base act of one of them did not lead me to doubt the others, nor did I withdraw from them my ill-judged and misplaced confidence until all and each of them proved by individual acts, the existence of a common disposition and movement to destroy my last hope of domestic peace Mrs Butler will one day deplore, if she has not done so already her too close connexion with those persons She made them her allies in her frantic warfare upon her own household, and thus far they have served her purposes, but their attachment has none of the qualities of true friendship, it yields subserviently to her will, and even to her opinions, wrong as they must often know them to be, having early discovered that those who wish to enjoy the charm of her association can only secure it by seeming to approve her worst follies Nor are they reliable, treachery is in their nature, and, when their own ends are to be answered, they will betray her with as little reluctance or disguise as they falsified their professions to me

On November 21, 1843, I made the first monthly payment of two hundred and eight dollars to Mr Theodore Sedgwick on Mrs Butler's account according to the arrangement in our respective letters of November 6 and 8 * From that time Mrs Butler assumed the separate occupation of her own apartments, and though under the same roof I never saw any thing of her My children went freely at all hours from my rooms into hers We had lived in this way for two months, when I was told that Mrs Butler spoke to others of the arrangement as a merely temporary one' saying that she intended suing for a divorce on the allegation of adultery, which, if successful would assign to her the custody of my children, that the requisite testimony only was wanting, and she expected soon to command it, as her friends were making such inquiries into my mode of life as would lead them to procure it This information, obtained in a way that left no doubt of the shameless schemes to which resort was had, gave me no uneasiness whatever I feared nothing in the shape of evidence and I knew that no law could invade my house and deprive me of my children, while I continued to protect and cherish them as a faithful and affectionate guardian

But I was also apprized that Mr Theodore Sedgwick was one of the peering and prying inquisitors in pursuit of evidence I could not credit this information. He had always in our relations acted with apparent frankness, and had so repeatedly expressed regret at our unhappy difficulties, with a desire to be

* Pages 98, 99

of service to both of us by his counsel and mediation, that I could not, with any reason or generosity, believe him to be playing a double part I was told of his having written to a person in London to ascertain and report any scandal that might have circulated about me during my residence there Although positively assured of this fact, my mind rejected it at first as impossible, but finally, to remove any doubt, I wrote to him frankly and briefly thus —

"*Philadelphia, January* 25, 1844.

" My dear Sedgwick.

" Did you write to Mr Lowndes in London, to ask him to give you information on any matter concerning my conduct while in London I would scarcely ask you such a question if I had not heard positively that you have done so, and I take the most direct way of ascertaining if it be incorrect or correct

" Yours, very truly,

" PIERCE BUTLER."

The following was his reply —

" *New York, February* 1, 1844

" My dear Butler,

" I regret that your letter of the 25th January has so long remained unanswered I received it this morning on my return from Albany, where I went last week

" I am in some doubt if I am at liberty to reply to your inquiry, and would prefer leaving it unanswered until next week, when I mean to be in Philadelphia, although, personally, I have no objection to answer at once. Any explanation that I have to make would be better and more satisfactorily made verbally. Whenever I do it, I suppose you will have no objection to let me know the name of your informant.

" This, perhaps, is all the reply that your letter now requires, but from a phrase which it contains, I infer the existence of an impression on your mind that I ought not to leave uncorrected. If I rightly apprehend that phrase, it implies that I was bound to communicate to you what passed between Mrs Butler and myself in regard to you, or that I was not at liberty to act in relation to the controversy between you and her without apprizing you of what I did. I think you cannot on reflection misunderstand my position in this matter. It is one in which I have never sought to intermeddle, in which I have interfered with great reluctance, and only in the hope of preventing an open rupture. But you cannot have forgotten that it is only as Mrs. Butler's friend and counsellor that I have acted. She first applied to me in regard to her property, and I advised the trust deed which was executed. She again applied to me in regard to her execution of conveyances, and I again advised her to execute such as you submitted for her signature. My agency was up to this time merely limited to advising her generally as to her rights and duties, and I had no intercourse with you on the subject but to apprize you of what I had done. In October last, when Mrs Butler discovered the letters which, in her opinion, gave her sufficient reason for insisting on an instant separation, she applied to me a third time, and I then, at *her* request, and as *her* friend and adviser saw you. We talked over the whole matter. I informed you of the efforts I had made to induce her to lay aside her intention of quitting your house, and stated to you distinctly the possibility of her filing a bill for a divorce on the ground of infidelity. After this conversation I cannot conceive you could have doubted that if most unfortunately, my efforts had been in vain, and Mrs Butler had applied to me professionally to enforce her rights by legal measures, that I should have considered myself not merely at liberty, but bound to assist her. Had I supposed any other impression existed in your mind, I should at once have sought to remove it, as I do now.

" The arrangement which resulted from that interview was purely temporary you refused to reduce any thing to writing, and Mrs. Butler and yourself both declined fixing any time for its continuance. I was agreed on as a sort of trustee for *her*, to receive and pay over her allowance

"Even more than this although from the nature of the case our conversation was private, and on private affairs, still *you* never placed the slightest confidence in me I knew nothing from you. You never gave me for a moment to understand, directly or indirectly, that you considered me otherwise than as *Mrs. Butler's* friend and legal adviser. I certainly then understood myself, as I do now, bound to assist her in every way in my power, but feeling as I did and do towards you, I was desirous to do every thing to prevent an open rupture So far as Mrs Butler's rights and interest could be protected without adverse measures, it was my duty and desire to prevent any interruption of the amicable relations which had previously existed between you and myself I hoped that, if possible, matters might not be brought to such a pass that I should be compelled to take any measures hostile to yourself

"I have said this much, perhaps unnecessarily, to prevent your remaining for a moment under an erroneous impression as to my view of my duties and responsibilities in this matter, though I can scarcely suppose that we have not perfectly understood each other

"I have now only to add, that I have done nothing throughout this whole matter, but with a single view to the best interests of yourself, your wife, and your children, and I have always considered that those interests could not be effectually served in any way but by keeping your family together

"I have all along been apprehensive that the moment must come when the nature of the controversy between you and Mrs. Butler would become such as to prevent my meeting you as we have heretofore done Whenever that period arrives, if arrive it must, I shall much regret it and particularly because it will greatly diminish my chances of usefulness to either of you

       " I am, very truly yours,

                             " THEODORE SEDGWICK

" PIERCE BUTLER, Esq , *Philadelphia* "

This hesitation of Mr Sedgwick to give an immediate and explicit answer to so straightforward a question, coupled with the long and evasive argumentation he professed to hang on a single, and to me undiscoverable phrase in my letter, instantly convinced me of his duplicity, and left not a vestige of doubt as to the light in which I must henceforth view him In order to make a position for himself he resorts to untruth he says " you cannot have forgotten that it is " only as Mrs Butler's friend and counsellor that I " have acted " That was not so Mrs Butler referred me to Mr Gerhard as her counsel,* and I refused to hold any communication with that gentleman as such, this I distinctly told Mr. Sedgwick when he visited me in my sick room for an answer to Mrs Butler's note of October 27, and at the same time I expressed my readiness to talk to him about my affairs, as I regarded him as a mutual friend, and he as distinctly told me that he wished me to consider him as such mutual friend, whose only desire was to do good to both, we accordingly entered upon the subject, and I conversed with him without reserve Had Mr. Sedgwick then avowed himself as the professional counsel of Mrs Butler, as he untruly asserts he did, I would have refused to see him, and that he knew

---

               * See Mrs Butler's note, p 97

very well, for why should I consent to receive him in that character, and refuse to see Mr Gerhard, to whom, personally, I had not the slightest objection and with whom I had always been on perfectly good terms' He further says, it was 'at *her* request and "as *her* friend and adviser that I saw you' And "you never gave me for a moment to understand, 'directly or indirectly, that you considered me other-"wise than as *Mrs Butler's* friend and legal adviser" In saying this Mr Sedgwick asserts what he is aware is untrue It is equally untrue when he says, "still "*you* never placed the slightest confidence in me I "knew nothing from you' On the contrary, I conversed with him in the most free and unsuspecting manner, and he admits that 'we talked over the whole matter,' and that "our conversation was private and on private affairs He says, 'I stated to 'you distinctly the possibility of her filing a bill for "a divorce on the ground of infidelity' yes, he said this, but he did not tell me that he was to be her advocate, and when he remarked that the 'letters dis-"covered by Mrs Butler in her opinion gave her suf-'ficient reason for insisting on an instant separation," I at once and without hesitation put those very letters into his hands, in the face of which he asserts that "I never placed the slightest confidence," in him, and that 'he knew nothing from me"

The history of these letters is this During my temporary absence in New York, Mrs Butler went to my secretary and examined my papers among them she found two letters, the seals of which had never been broken, she broke the seals and read the letters, she found them to be old, written several years before, without signatures, and apparently in the handwriting of a female I had never opened or read them On my return from New York she handed them to me and acknowledged what she had done I was very much provoked, and deeming her act in breaking the seals as unjustifiable as her searching among my papers was indelicate and unwarrantable, I refused to give her any explanation whatever respecting them She was incensed at my opinion of her conduct, and upon these incidents, and these alone, has vented her suspicions and imputations of infidelity When Mr Sedgwick referred to these letters in our conversation I immediately gave them to him, to let him see that their contents would not sustain the inference she had drawn from them He too must have thought so, for they were never called for by her counsel, as they certainly might have been if judged to import criminality It is to this circumstance Mrs Butler refers in her ' *Narrative*" when she says—"In consequence of discovering, in October, " 1843, as I believed. that he had been guilty of a ' breach of the primary obligations of the marriage " contract, at an early, and what to me had been a less " unhappy period of my married life—although I do " not assert such to have been the case as matter of fact, ' forasmuch as I have not legal proof thereof—and in " consequence of my communicating that belief to him " with the evidence on which I had adopted it, the last " hope of reunion became extinguished, our inter- " course as husband and wife totally ceased, the rela- " tion itself practically terminated, and thereupon, an " arrangement of separation was entered into, under " which we continued to live as I have above stated "

These two violated letters, never read by me, are absolutely all that she and her allies, the Sedgwicks, ever have been able to conjure up in support of their oft repeated charge of infidelity

Mr Sedgwick's reply having fully manifested his real attitude and character, I wrote to him as follows

"*Philadelphia, February* 4, 1844

" Sir,

" Your letter of February 1st was received yesterday You decline answering at once my inquiry, and I am not surprised at your refusal The new character in which you now choose to exhibit yourself renders it necessary to call special pleading and equivocation to your aid and admonishes me not to expect from you in future the candour and frankness that should characterize the intercourse of friends For the first time you there declare yourself exclusively the legal adviser of Mrs Butler, in what you are pleased to term her 'controversy' with me Have you forgotten, Sir, that when you handed me the note from Mrs Butler, in which she requested a separation and in which she referred me to Mr Gerhard as her legal adviser, that I then expressed to you my determination to hold no communication with any lawyer on the subject, but that I should have no objection to confer with you as the mutual friend of Mrs. Butler and myself? Have you also forgotten your distinct assurance that you acted only in the capacity of mutual friend? You cannot have so treacherous a memory but now that you feel yourself detected in a violation of all honour and decency, and can no longer conceal your designs against my domestic peace, you announce yourself as the counsellor, forsooth, of the other party. You have sought to obtain materials from the vilest sources for the purpose of fomenting dissention in my family your own conscience should teach you that a faithful legal adviser, who consults the real interests of his client, should not lend himself to the angry passions and jealous fancies of an excited woman, and should hesitate to encourage in such delicate matters a recourse to legal tribunals. Even where the proofs of a husband's infidelity are undeniable, any honest lawyer and true friend would be anxious to soothe the indignant feelings of the injured wife, and to restore the harmony which had previously existed between the parties; but in the present case where no evidence of unfaithfulness can be adduced, I hold the conduct of that man deserving of the severest reprehension, who, acting under the pretence of sympathy for imaginary wrongs, or under a hypocritical affectation of professional duty, seeks to establish by the most infamous practices a conviction in the mind of his ill-advised client of her husband's unworthiness, and to confirm by positive testimony what was before only a matter of vague suspicion. To conclude, Sir, I have only to say that I consider the tone of your letter impertinent, and the matter irrelative to the subject on which I thought proper to address you, and that I look upon it as a laboured effort on your part to define the new position which my recent call upon you has forced you to assume. You will understand that in future I can hold no further communication with you on any subject whatever.

                  " I am, Sir,

                         " Your obedient servant,

                                " PIERCE BUTLER.

' THEODORE SEDGWICK, Esq., *New York* "

Notwithstanding the unequivocal and peremptory tone of the foregoing, Mr Sedgwick ventured to address me again; but I returned his letter unopened. I sent it to a friend in New York to hand back to him with the seal unbroken, which was done, as I learned from the following —

" New York, February 9, 1844.

" My dear Butler,

"I have just delivered to Mr Sedgwick, personally, the letter which you enclosed to me for that purpose, of course without any discussion or conversation If I can be of any further service to you, do not hesitate to call upon me

" Ever faithfully yours,

" BEVERLEY ROBINSON, Jr.

" PIERCE BUTLER, Esq "

This ended all intercourse between Mr Theodore Sedgwick and myself

I continued to pay monthly to Mr Gerhard the sum of two hundred and eight dollars for Mrs Butler's separate use she had her own lodgings and table, saw as much of her children as I did, and experienced no sort of interference from me After many years of patient trial, I had slowly and finally exhausted the cup of hope, and had reached the conviction that to live with her without degradation, perpetual strife, and wretchedness, was an impossibility she was absolutely impracticable kindness did not win, forbearance did not conciliate, and control was defied I now pursued a different course As she had voluntarily gone from me, I determined henceforth to let her follow unchecked her own will in her own way, I furnished a confessedly ample allowance, and she was as free and uncontrolled in all her actions as the wildest spirit could desire

Having thus accorded to her an independent position, I trusted to secure for myself a greater degree of peace than I had found it possible to obtain since my union with her, and as I left her entirely to herself, I had reasonable grounds for expecting that she would cease making it the business and enjoyment of her life to harass me. My expectations however were not realized, she was as little satisfied in this condition of things as in any other that preceded it, and she showed no greater degree of contentment in her new attitude of unfettered freedom than when cramped by what she denominated my tyranny. Leagued with confederates, whose double-dealing I had detected, she and they spread abroad imputations against me as defamatory as they were unfounded. not only was the slang of infidelity pertinaciously reiterated but in their zeal to injure they did not scruple to accuse me of conduct of even a more serious character, and to soil their own lips with calumnies so gross that I cannot here even allude to them. No expedient was left untried to discover evidence with which to corroborate the charge of infidelity, but, failing in this, they nevertheless resolved to compel belief by constant repetition, and, by dint of unwearied efforts, they succeeded.

During this vile persecution, for it was really nothing less, and when society fairly rang with my monstrosities of conduct, I remained perfectly quiet, I did nothing, spoke to no one on the subject, not even to my relatives or most intimate friends, and, indeed, made no attempt to stem the current of slander setting so steadily and strongly against me. This course was, perhaps, not a prudent one, for by my silence and their calumnious loquacity my character was certainly injured, and my social position seriously affected. Persons who had always been friendly and cordial were now, when met, cold and distant and many who knew me well enough to discredit any thing to my disadvantage were yet unable to vindicate me against charges so boldly advanced, because I did not furnish them with the appropriate means: I bore with patience all the odium heaped upon my shoulders Although three lawyers were employed against me, I took no legal advice whatever, nor did I seek counsel from a single person I was silent my assailant was my wife, and I was content to bear all the injury she sought to inflict

But if I had wished to pursue a different course, and to defend myself, it would have been hardly possible then to do so, for though aware that serious accusations were disseminated against me, I did not accurately learn what those accusations were it is only since, and from time to time, that they have been fully disclosed to me Nor is it ever easy to repel the assaults of misrepresentation and calumny, however unfounded, they leave impressions which it is exceedingly difficult, if not impossible, wholly to efface Slander is too subtle to be followed through all its tortuous courses, it penetrates into regions where refutation can never find its way From the attacks of an open enemy, an upright man has nothing to fear, he knows at once their aim and force, and can disprove them against such attacks too, one's previous character and life are a broad shield But when his enemy emerges from his own household, and when his wife, as if driven from her stand at his side, becomes his assailant, he is powerless It is so natural to woman to cling to and praise those who belong to her, that if a wife turns accuser against her husband, we easily believe that she has some cause for doing so, and the ready sympathy that every female, thought to be ill treated, finds in her own sex soon secures a host of partisans those who were friends before are bound still closer to her, and those who were indifferent, or perhaps averse, marshal themselves warmly in her favour under an instinctive and generous impulse Mrs Butler's imaginary though loudly vented wrongs soon gathered round her more friends than she had been able to attract when we were supposed to be living happily together

It was not only in this country that calumny was employed to undermine and injure me, it was used in England also, and the same efforts were there made to create the impression that my wife had been treated with harshness and cruelty I am constrained to say that those who knew me on the other side of the Atlantic were more candid and impartial than many on this Upon hearing the stories, they wrote to me for explanations, and evinced a desire that I should communicate with them on the subject for they were not quite disposed implicitly to adopt all that was said against me, merely because Mrs Butler was its author Many letters passed between us, and I endeavoured to disabuse their minds I found them not only considerate and fair, but unwilling to decide upon a case in which the facts could not be otherwise than partially represented to them One or two of their letters will be enough to insert here, others will be given in subsequent pages Mr Kemble, the father of Mrs Butler, addressed me thus —

Q

" My dear Pierce,

" I did not answer your letter by the first mail, in the hope I might hear that you and Fanny had come to a better understanding, and now, I have nothing to say but that these unhappy differences make me very miserable   What can I, what can any body, what ought any body to say between man and wife?   All may see their altered conduct towards each other, but who shall presume to divine the causes of that conduct and to judge between them?   Mutual forbearance is the only remedy to be resorted to in such a case   and my dear friend, by that I hope, in a short time, to hear that your quarrels are ended, and that you are once more living at least on friendly terms   Think what the consequences of these disputes, if they continue, must be to your dear children   to whom, at this early period of their lives, a mother's care is so inestimable, and as the greater power is with you, remember that the greater share of forbearance should accompany it and by the exercise of that win back the affections of your wife and with them the approval of all upright men

*   *   *   *   " You will be glad to hear that my health is quite restored and that I am better than I have been for years   God bless you, my son, I long to hear that you are reconciled to poor Fanny, and will not renounce the hope of so much comfort to my declining years

" Believe me yours, affectionately,

" C KEMBLE "

Mr Sartoris, the husband of Mrs Butler's sister, wrote as follows —

" My dear Pierce,

*   *   *   *   " Adelaide told me to add that late circumstances have made it so painful for her to write to you, that she preferred communicating through me I should not wish you to think that in so doing she is actuated by any feeling of resentment, for I feel certain that is not the case, and I hope you will yourself understand that under the present circumstances writing to you would be very painful to her without reference to passing any judgment on the state of things between yourself and her sister as for myself God knows, I pass none, but content myself with hoping that a better time may come than the present for the children's sake, for Fanny's, and for your own

' Believe me, yours ever

"E. J. Sartoris '

The sentences omitted, where stars appear, in the above letters of Mr Kemble and Mr Sartoris, refer merely to trifling matters of business, in no way connected with the portions quoted

I have heretofore stated that on my return from England, in May, 1843, I took my family to a boarding-house, and I continued to reside at the same place until, after the lapse of more than a year, a house of my own was engaged On beginning arrangements for removal, I received a note from Mr Meredith, one of Mrs Butler's professional counsel —

" Dear Sir,

"I am desirous of having an interview with you in the course of to-day, and I will do myself the pleasure of calling on you at any hour you may name, or will receive you at any time that may suit you between seven and ten o'clock, this evening

"Very truly yours,

W. M. Meredith

" Pierce Butler, Esq. '   · May 1, 1844

I called on Mr Meredith and was informed by him that Mrs Butler had heard of my intention to leave my present lodgings, was unwilling to be separated from her children, and had no objection to accompany them to the house I had taken

He also wished to know where I proposed to pass the summer I answered this latter inquiry at once, and promised to write to him the next day on the former subject I did so

" Dear Sir,

" At your request I inform you that my intention is to move, in the course of this month into the house I have taken About the first of July I shall go to Newport for two months.

" It has never been a wish of mine to separate my children from their mother, the partial separation that has existed between them since November last, has been the consequence of Mrs Butler's ' determination to be separated' from me, as formerly expressed in her note to me, dated 27th October, 1843.

" You now inform me that it is Mrs Butler's wish to remain with her children, and that if I propose to her to accompany them into the house I have taken, that she will do so I shall not thwart her wish, provided she is prepared to conduct herself in such a manner as an inmate of every family is bound to do

" Since November last, she has been in the constant practice of abusing me in the strongest language to every person that would listen to her, and her most intimate associates have been chosen from persons who have taken a violent and bitter part against me Should she again become a member of my family, and an inmate of my house, all this must cease

" In order that she may be under the same roof with her children, I propose to her to accompany them to the house I have provided for their home It is necessary, however, in order to protect myself, and to insure domestic privacy, that certain conditions be annexed to this proposal These are, that all acquaintance and intercourse, of whatever kind, whether by word or letter, shall, at once, and for ever, cease between Mrs Butler and every member of the Sedgwick family, and that hereafter she shall treat them, in every respect, as entire strangers and as if she had never known them

"That Mrs Butler will not keep up an acquaintance with any person that I may disapprove of, and that in her future intercourse with her friends in this country and in England, she will not mention any circumstance which may occur in my house or family, and that she will, in like manner, cease to speak of me in terms of reprobation and reproach

"If you will reflect on this, you will perceive that I have stipulated for nothing unusual or unnecessary, but only require what is absolutely essential to the well-being and right government of every family.

"If Mrs Butler considers her duty to her children paramount to all other considerations, she will have no difficulty in acceding to this proposal, in which case I need scarcely say to you, that I will endeavour to make her residence with her children as comfortable as it can be, whilst her excited state of feeling against me continues

"I must beg you to let me have a definite answer to this proposal within two days, I am making arrangements for going into the house, which will be modified by Mrs Butler's determination

" Yours truly,

" PIERCE BUTLER

"Wm M Meredith, Esq."   " May 2, 1844

I was replied to by the following —

" Dear Sir,

"I have to acknowledge the receipt of your note of the second in-

stant, which I have submitted to Mrs Butler for her consideration
She will not accept the conditions which you have named in it

"Very truly yours,

"W M MEREDITH

"PIERCE BUTLER, Esq"   "May 5, 1844

After receiving this peremptory rejection of my
proposal, I went on with preparations for a change of
quarters, nor did I hear more from Mrs Butler, or
her counsel, for some time

Let me be pardoned for introducing at this appropriate stage of my statement a letter received from the
Rev Mr Furness —

"Dear Sir,

"As your friend, and the friend of Mrs. Butler, will you permit
me to ask whether any friendly offices of mine can be of any use?
I make this request entirely without the knowledge of Mrs Butler,
and with a repugnance at the idea of interfering, so strong, that only
a most earnest desire to serve you both urges me to overcome it
The friendly relations that subsisted between your mother and myself embolden me in making an offer of service, which our personal
relations, however friendly, would hardly seem to justify   I feel
deeply the delicacy of the affair, and the impropriety, not to say impossibility of judging justly without the entire confidence and consent
of both parties   Should it be agreeable to you to use my services,
I would be happy to see you at my house, or call upon you at yours

"With cordial good wishes,

"Your friend,

"W H FURNESS.

"Pine street, June 6, 1844.

"PIERCE BUTLER, Esq"

I sent the subjoined answer —

"Dear Sir,

"Had I thought it of any use to seek the advice and assistance of any person in my domestic troubles, I should have turned to you as the friend most likely to aid me. I have consulted no one, nor do I believe that good would result from my doing so. My course for the future is determined on, and I have no expectation that any thing will occur to alter it. Had Mrs. Butler any reason for her strange conduct—had she the slightest cause to drive her into her past treatment of me, I could have some hope for the future. I would, in that case, ask for forgiveness, and I might hope to obtain it from a woman's forgiving nature. But her resentment against me has been so entirely unprovoked, and her persecution of me so bitter, that I have no right to expect anything from the future, but a repetition of the past.

' I solemnly declare that my treatment of her has been just and kind, and my conscience fully acquits me of any one act towards her, of which a reasonable woman could justly complain.

"That you may not be altogether unapprized of my feelings on this painful subject, and that you may know what bad influences have been at work to destroy my domestic peace, I send for you to read copies of two letters, one written a few days ago, the other last February.

"Consideration for my children, and for the memory of my mother, makes me wish that those who knew her should not rest under false impressions of my unworthiness, and that they should not believe me capable of many things which have been charged against me by one who, under all circumstances, should have been the protector and defender of my character, and not my slanderer and defamer.

"Believe that I appreciate and am grateful to you for the kind intentions with which you have written to me, and should it appear that the counsel of a friend may be of use, I will have no hesitation in seeking your aid

"Sincerely and gratefully,

"Your friend,

"PIERCE BUTLER

"Rev Mr Furness" "June 7, 1844.

Delays consequent upon building an addition to my house, retarded my removal to it until the first of August, 1844 Before effecting that, however, and while still at the boarding-house, I again heard from Mr Meredith —

"My dear Sir,

"Mrs Butler requests me to ascertain whether, in lieu of the conditions proposed by you, you will be satisfied with a promise on her part, never in any way to any one again to advert to the circumstances of your past life together, never to refer to them by word or letter to any human being, in short to bury them utterly She states that she is ready to pledge herself thus far for the past, and thinks she shall be assisted in following the same course for the future by having your relations, if you live under the same roof, so well defined and settled, as to leave as little occasion as possible for either giving, or taking offence These relations to be arranged only in reference to her intercourse with her children. Mrs Butler adds, that should these proposals be accepted, the present provision for her maintenance will, she presumes, be done away with, and with regard to any other arrangement for her expenditure, she is willing to abide by your will upon the subject

"I am, dear sir, very truly yours,

"W. M. MEREDITH

"PIERCE BUTLER, Esq" "June 13, 1844

This proposal appeared so like an attempt to equivocate and trifle with me, that I treated it thus —

"Dear Sir,

"There is no 'circumstance or act of my 'past life' which I desire 'to bury.' The slander and defamation which have been heaped on me for the past year, have already done me and my children all the harm that can be done. I care not if they be discontinued, or still longer indulged in.

"Your note of 5th May was taken as a final answer to my proposal, and I have since taken my measures accordingly. It seems unnecessary to have any further correspondence on this subject.

"I am yours, very truly,

"PIERCE BUTLER.

"W. M. MEREDITH, Esq."   "June 14, 1844.

Mrs. Butler's proposition, as developed through Mr. Meredith, amounted in reality to nothing at all. After having indulged to exhaustion in vituperation for nearly a year, and done me all the injury in her power, she was now ready to promise to say nothing more about "the past." her poison was administered, and she was willing to let its work be done without further effort. But what pledge did she offer for the future? "She thinks she shall be assisted in follow- "ing the same course for the future by having your "relations, if you live under the same roof, so well "defined and settled, as to leave as little occasion as "possible for either giving, or taking offence. These 'relations to be arranged only in reference to her in- "tercourse with her children.' The meaning of which was simply, that her visits, correspondence, and intercourse were not to be interfered with. that

R

she was to be free as heretofore, to select her friends
and associates from among my avowed and bitter enemies that she was to have them congregated, if she
so pleased, in my house and on her part she "thinks"
she would be able ' for the future ' to forbear slan-
dering me These were the terms suggested by her
in lieu of mine ' terms which appeared to her such
" as might satisfy any reasonable human being '* I
knew her and understood them too well to be duped

Mrs Butler did not renew her application to reside
under the same roof with her children for more than
four months after I had established them in their
new home On December 10, 1844 the Rev Mr
Furness handed me a communication from her —

" I have committed this to the care of our excellent mutual friend,
Mr Furness, in order that it may reach you in the least distasteful
manner possible , as I do not wish any thing in the mode of my addressing you to interfere with the object I have in view. I am induced by the most serious considerations to make one more endeavour to regain my proper position towards my children I will lay
my reasons before you, that you may not misapprehend me My
sister and several of my friends in England, adjure me with the
utmost earnestness, to make another overture to you , believing that
you are accessible to a reasonable one. For their sakes, and to
leave them no doubt as to my course of conduct, and the motives I
am actuated by, I take this step I am also told by many persons
who have direct and indirect communication with you, that you have
expressed regret at my separation from my children It is very difficult indeed to ascertain the precise truth of such reports, passed as

* Mrs Butler's " *Narrative,*" page 6

they are from mouth to mouth, but because I know several people who are, I believe, as kindly disposed towards you as towards myself, who entertain this opinion. I will not neglect to ascertain if an impression so favourable to my own wishes be true. My chief inducement, however, in addressing you, and one that makes all other considerations light, is the conviction that it is my duty to make one more effort—a most earnest one—to obtain from you the restoration of my rights over my children. Your own assurance given to Mr Gerhard, that I should see my children daily, was infringed at the very outset by your taking them to Newport, and preventing my going thither under a threat of keeping them all the summer in town if I did so. Since their return to Philadelphia, they have both of them been repeatedly kept from me, and the seven hours a week which you yourself appointed as my portion of intercourse with my children, have been curtailed, at your pleasure, until I have not the slightest reason to reckon upon the arrangement. Within the last three weeks you have, moreover, deliberately determined that Sarah is to omit her visit to me regularly once a fortnight, thus not only accidentally, and for occasional reasons, but of set purpose and by your own arrangement—the little intercourse you professed to intend I should have with my children, is reduced to still less. On the other hand, although my allotted time with them has been thus sometimes infringed upon, and sometimes altered so as to occasion me the greatest inconvenience, I have never been able to obtain, though I once or twice have requested it, that the hour of their visit should be altered in order to accommodate me, nor have I once been allowed their society on Saturday, their holiday, though I have sent to request it repeatedly, and though they have been allowed to spend it indifferently with any friends or acquaintance who invited them and occasionally have passed the greater part of their holiday afternoon, in which their society was invariably denied me, in rambling about with no other guardianship but that of a very young and ignorant Irish servant girl. This miserable and interrupted intercourse with my children, instead of contributing, in any degree, to my comfort or happiness, has, through its dependence upon your will, become a source of constant suffering, disappointment and bitterness to me, and though I would endure all the pain that such wretched communion with my children gives me, if they were to derive the slightest benefit from it, I am so perfectly convinced that no good accrues to them from my unfortunate position, and the sad and meagre seasons of intercourse with me allowed them, that an effort to render our relations more what they should be, is as much to be made for their sakes as mine   *   *   *   *   I have known that this must hereafter be the case, and indeed have hoped to receive from my child's sense of right some reward in future years for all the bitterness I have endured for her sake, yet I have ever scrupulously forborne to mention your name to her otherwise than with the respect which I hope you may be able to inspire her with   But independently of all these sad causes for thinking it expedient to alter my present position, there is a more serious one still, which, embracing the highest welfare of my child, affects me more than any mere consideration of the sadness of the lot of these young creatures—girls—deprived of the care of a mother, which, I believe, no one has ever yet thought of considering second in efficiency to that of any possible substitute   *   *   *   *

These are my motives for again addressing you   I will now propose to you a mode of remedying these evils, which I most sincerely hope you will consent to, and for which, failing your acceding to my proposal, I must seek others infinitely to be deprecated. I earnestly request and entreat you to permit me admission to the home of my children upon the following understanding   an entire abstinence on my part from all reference to the past, an engagement that I will publish nothing without your consent, and that I will neither write nor speak of you to any one soever while I remain under your roof, and will hold you of course at liberty to pursue your own career without comment or interference of mine   Moreover, I presume, I need not add that I do not expect to see or receive in your house any person or persons who may be obnoxious to you As I make this last appeal to you from the most imperative sense of duty, and upon the most mature consideration, I solemnly assure you that I will keep these conditions, not only to the letter, but in the spirit of peace and rectitude My children and my obligations to them constrain me to this measure, and for their sakes I adjure you to receive my proposal "

The suppressions indicated by asterisks, in the above letter, are observations concerning my children Mrs Butler thought it proper to omit these from her printed "*Narrative*," and, therefore, they are not here reinstated

As I invariably refused to hold direct communication with Mrs Butler during this period of absence from her family, my answer to the foregoing was made to the Rev Mr Furness —

" Dear Sir,

" The communication that Mrs Butler has thought proper to address to me, and which was delivered to me by yourself contains the expression of a seemingly sincere desire to resume her duty to her children, a duty that she deliberately abandoned fourteen months ago, and which she has entirely neglected during the whole of the subsequent time. Seven months ago I wrote to Mr Meredith, and named the conditions on which Mrs Butler was free to become again an inmate of my family; she then rejected them without hesitation, and now proposes other terms I can find no reason for any change in the conditions stated to Mr Meredith, and if Mrs Butler be sincere in her desire to live with her children she can have no hesitation in agreeing to them

" The causes which existed at that time to oblige me to stipulate such terms, are still in force, and it would not be possible for Mrs Butler to live in my house, without the most rigid observance of those terms If she determine to accede to them, I will endeavour to make such changes in the arrangement of the household, as will enable her to live in the family She must bear in mind, however, that in consequence of her desertion of the children, I have been obliged for a year past to assume the entire direction of them, and that the arrangements I have made for their studies and education, must in no way be interfered with

"It would be well for Mrs Butler to refer to the letter addressed to Mr Meredith, and again to weigh the precise terms proposed in it, she will find that I require her to renounce ' at once and for ever,' all communication with those low-bred, vulgar meddlers, the Sedgwicks

"I should be glad to know her determination without delay, as a state of uncertainty on the subject is by no means agreeable

"Yours, very sincerely,

"PIERCE BUTLER.

"Rev WM. H FURNESS"   "Dec. 13, 1844

The very next day came the following note —

"Dear Sir,

"I handed your letter to Mrs. Butler, and she requests me to inform you that the step proposed to her in going into your house upon such terms is so serious and important that she must decline giving a positive answer upon the subject for two or three days at least, such a determination requiring the utmost consideration

"Very truly, your friend,

· W H FURNESS

"Dec 14, 1844 "

I was, I must confess, greatly surprised and immediately addressed Mr Furness —

                 ' *Saturday evening, Dec* 14, 1844.

" Dear Sir,

   " Your note of this evening has caused a painful change in the
feeling produced by Mrs Butler's letter I believed her sincere
when she wrote ' I earnestly request and entreat you to permit me
'admission to the home of my children, and again ' As I make this
'last appeal to you from the most imperative sense of duty, and upon
'the most mature consideration, I solemnly assure you that I will keep
'these conditions, not only to the letter, but in the spirit of peace and
'rectitude, my children and my obligations to them constrain me to
'this measure, and for their sake I adjure you to receive my proposal.'
I was full of hope The home of my children seemed already
brighter and happier for them, for I thought it was again to be blessed by a mother's presence and care I hoped that better feelings actuated Mrs Butler, that she was resolved to repress her enmity to
me, and to make her own prejudices yield to her children's good
Her desire to be with her children seemed as real as it was natural
What can I think now ? She has had seven months to consider the
terms of my proposal, and she still requires more time You have
repeatedly assured me that she was ready to come into my house
upon the conditions required of her She herself asks permission
to come into it, and when she is told she is free to come, she draws
back, and says she must consider about it Is this sincere? She
abandons the most solemn of earthly duties—she separates herself
from her children for no cause but hate of their father—for more
than a year she leaves them motherless—and then speaks of her return to this sacred duty as ' a determination requiring the utmost
consideration,' a step so serious and important that she must decline giving a positive answer for two or three days at least ' The
deepest obligations of life are in a moment violated by her, but she

requires time and consideration to make up her mind to resume those obligations, and to return to her neglected children. What did she mean by her letter?—What by her 'appeal' to me, 'made from the most imperative sense of duty, and upon the most mature consideration?' Did she expect me to reject her prayer and thus afford her a pretext to cast fresh odium upon me? To say, 'he shuts his doors against me, and denies me shelter under the same roof with my children?' Indeed, her conduct at present looks very much as if such was her design She has deceived you by telling you that she could consent to any condition rather than be separated from her children. Why does she not instantly consent? I impose no new conditions—nothing but what she has already declared she was ready to assent to She has led you to believe that her objection to the conditions imposed last spring, and then rejected, was not now the obstacle that kept her from her children, but that my will was the cause of it, in short, that the separation did not depend upon her, but upon me, that my doors were shut against her because she had not yielded her assent within the specified time Why, then, does she hesitate to accept the same proposal which is now renewed, and treat it as if it contained fresh stipulations, too burdensome to be agreed to without the utmost consideration? Does this accord with her professions? Is it not an attempt to fix upon me the stigma of cruelly separating her from her children?

"That which I received as sincere in her letter, does not appear so any longer. She may take as many days as she chooses, to consider if it be right to return to her duty as a mother, but I shall receive her into my house with far different feelings from those I was prepared to entertain if she had not hesitated about coming I must believe any resolution she may now come to, to return and live with her children, will be made for expediency, and not solely from a sincere desire to be with them.

"Yours, very sincerely,

"PIERCE BUTLER.

"Rev. WM. H. FURNESS."

In order to cloak and excuse this reluctance to live
in the house with her children, if obliged to observe
becoming rules of domestic conduct, she pretends that
I had imposed " new conditions,' which were " a
" grievous increase of the hardship of the former
" terms + And she adds, " he professed to assent to
" my proposal upon the conditions he had formerly
" proposed to me, but he really added to his
" former terms, that I should in no way participate
" in the care, or control, or management of my chil-
" dren, if I came into his house "+ This is an obvious perversion of a passage in my letter, the words
are —" She must bear in mind, however, that in con-
" sequence of her desertion of the children, I have
" been obliged for a year past to assume the entire
' direction of them, and that the arrangements 1 have
" made for their studies and education must in no way
" be interfered with "‡

The sentence is not liable to the interpretation she
endeavours to impute to it in fact, there was no such
stipulation at all insisted upon, for in the draft of
conditions prescribed by me, and to which she put her
signature, the children are not even mentioned, and
the terms were precisely those contained in my letter
of May 2, 1844, to Mr Meredith, which she at that
date promptly and flatly rejected §

Mr Furness replied to my letter —

" Dear Sir,

" In reply to your note just received, I will merely state my own
conviction that if, when Mrs Butler's letter produced so happy an

* Mrs Butler's ' Narrative," p 11   † Idem, pp 8 9
‡ See page 134   § See page 124

S

impression upon you, you had met it in its own spirit, and replied, 'Come, come upon the conditions you propose, and I will rely upon the promise you so solemnly make to keep them,' there would have been, I apprehend, no hesitation, not the slightest delay. But in referring her back to the letter to Mr Meredith, you proposed other conditions, conditions which she might indeed *promise* to observe, and try to observe *to the letter*, but in the possibility of observing them *in the spirit*, she has no belief. In all that she offers to do, she is, I believe, thoroughly sincere. Besides, your letter to me in answer to her letter to you produced even on my mind the painful impression that her letter had not had the slightest effect upon you.

" Your friend,

" W. H. Furness

" P Butler, Esq."   " *Dec* 16, 1844

It was quite natural that Mr Furness, or any one else, ignorant of my previous and various experiments, should think me too rigid in exacting these conditions and his remarks in no respect surprised me, but had he known a tithe of the disappointed hopes and broken pledges to which I had already been subjected, he would scarcely have expected me even to affect reliance on Mrs Butler's good faith, or simple promises

Two days elapsed, and Mr Furness transmitted to me the following letter from Mrs Butler —

" *Dec.* 18, 1844.

" Dear Mr. Furness,

" Will you be good enough to inform Mr Butler that I hold myself in readiness to profit by his permission of living with my children at his convenience The terms he imposes upon me I will keep to the best of my ability while I reside under his roof At the same time, I must deny utterly the charge of hatred which Mr. Butler brings against me, inasmuch as I have no such feeling towards any human being and also enter my solemn protest against the accusation of having deserted my children, to preserve my proper relation with whom has always been my most earnest desire and endeavour

" I am yours ever, truly,

" FANNY "

And I immediately wrote him —

" Dear Sir,

" Mrs Butler having at length concluded to return to her children, I shall lose no time in making the necessary arrangements for her coming into the house There are some questions of minor importance, but yet of consequence, about which I should like to speak with you in order to have a clear understanding on the subject. If you will do me the favour to call here, at any time convenient to yourself, I shall feel much obliged to you

" Yours, very sincerely,

" PIERCE BUTLER

" Rev. WM H FURNESS."   " Dec 18 1844

There are, no doubt many persons who entertain the opinion that the conditions imposed as preliminary to Mrs Butler's resuming a place in my habitation were unnecessarily restrictive and harsh, but I beg it may be borne in mind under what circumstances I acted. I had long essayed every art and means of conciliation the love I bore her I once thought could cease only at death it struggled long against the bitter overthrow of every hope and vision of happiness, and I would cheerfully have sacrificed fortune, or life itself, to awaken one feeling in her heart which might lead her to contemplate truly and avert the sad waste she was making of existence, and of all its precious opportunities and uses. But at length she fairly wore out, crushed, and extinguished my affection. the blessings by which we might have remained surrounded were first embittered and finally blasted. all was at an end between us. there was no desire on the part of either to be reunited, that indeed was impossible, for no trace of attachment lingered in the breast of either, we were no longer one, not even formal friends, she had become my calumniator, and exulted over the victim of her envenomed slander.

These conditions, then, were not dictated to a wife, for she had thrown away that exalted character, they were necessary to self-protection, to secure, if possible, the dignity and privacy of home, to entrench domestic scenes and incidents from the misrepresentation and obloquy to which Mrs Butler, in her eagerness to confirm the prejudices of others against me, had never hesitated to resort. I must confess I could devise no plan for these purposes more moderate or more efficient, after what I had already undergone, than that of exacting absolute silence upon such topics.

With respect to the requirement, that she should "not keep up an acquaintance with any person of whom I might disapprove," it had, as was mutually known, application only to the Sedgwick family, and to one other person, from intercourse with whom she, of her own accord, has since abstained. Her admirers in this city are, as they have given me reason to discern, made *strongly averse to myself* by impressions derived from her, but, as they never interfered improperly with my private relations or affairs, I entertain towards them no unkind feeling whatever, and could never have the least desire other than to sanction and encourage their free and frequent visits at my house while she was there Still, as it was impossible to foresee to what new allies she might extend her confidence, and how far they might prove intrusive and objectionable, I thought it safer and less invidious at once to make the provision general

I considered these rules, indeed, more in the light of a reasonable and decorous compromise, which, for the sake of our children, would make it possible for us to live in the same house, and to maintain, if not entirely harmonious, at least decent and pacific relations It is quite certain from letters now in my possession, that these conditions were not regarded by some of Mrs Butler s family and friends in England as either uncalled for or too stringent In support of this assertion, I adduce one or two of these letters

London, Feb 4, 1845.

" My dear Pierce,

" Your last letter afforded us great satisfaction it gave us great joy to know that Fanny was once more under the same roof with her children however much—and nobody will admit the fact more readily than myself—she may have drawn misfortune on her own shoulders by the rashness of her proceedings, the penalty was so severe that we could not help feeling the greatest sympathy for her unfortunate position and I earnestly hope that nothing will occur to alter her present situation, so much the most advantageous for your children, and so much the most respectable for all parties Against your conditions I confess I have nothing to urge Total separation from the Sedgwicks was, I agree with you, indispensable I have

never ceased to lament Fanny's connexion with people, who, in my
opinion, have always given her the very worst possible advice, and
I think the other condition required nothing but what every woman
is bound to do in order to preserve peace and quiet in her interior
At the same time, I earnestly hope that for the sake of continuing
the present desirable state of things, you will endeavour to promote
her comfort as much as possible, and especially allow her a fair share
in the general care and education of her children. this is a right,
which, with all her errors, she has done nothing to forfeit, and I entreat you to recollect that in depriving her of, or unnecessarily interfering with, the exercise of that right, you would almost entirely
counterbalance the good you have done by allowing her to live in the
house you would thereby awaken her sense of justice, which forms
such a strong feature of her character, and you would remove the
natural vent from a mind already so restlessly active She has generosity among her good qualities, and I believe the appearance of a
certain confidence reposed in her would do more towards softening
her disposition, than severity and control which only serve to irritate her After all, in this world *we must cut our cloth, §c*, and
mothers have feelings with regard to the children of their womb,
which we men are hardly able to *realize*, as you say in America;
add to that such a character as Fanny's, and how unwise and unfair
it would be to wound her in this most sensitive point

  " I know Charles Greville has written you by this post, and as I am
sure he will have said all that can be said upon the subject, much
better than I possibly can do, I will spare you any further eloquence
of mine

  " You had much better all come over here next Spring.

      " Believe me, ever,

          " Your sincere friend and well-wisher,

              "E J Sartoris "

In the letter mentioned by Mr Sartoris, as having been written to me by Mr Charles Greville, that gentleman says, "I do think it impossible to revive feel- "ings, which have been so wounded and crushed, but "there is no reason why you should not live together ' as friends, and cultivate relations sufficient for all social purposes, and for the welfare of the children "As to the terms you presented I think you did very "wisely and I rejoice that she at last agreed to ac- "cept them "*

Some time having elapsed after Mrs Butler had signified her readiness to rejoin her children, Mr Furness, at her request, inquired by note when her rooms would be ready   I replied by the following —

"Dear Sir,

"I beg you to excuse me for not sooner replying to your letter   I have been much annoyed at the delay in the arrangements of the house, as it might seem to be intentional   such, however, is not the case, for I am most desirous to have my family in a more settled state than it is at present   The cause of the delay is simply this   When I came into this house, nothing more was done to it in the way of painting, papering, and furnishing than was absolutely neces- sary at the time   It was not until I set about putting it in order for Mrs Butler's reception that I was aware how little had been done, and how much yet remained to be done   Furnishing a house, or even half of one, is not the work of a day, and more time has passed since we first spoke together upon the subject, than, at that time, I could have supposed possible.   I regret that I cannot, for yet a few days, inform you of the precise time when Mrs Butler's rooms will

* Mr Greville s letter is dated London, February 1, 1845

be ready for her   I will do so as soon as I can ascertain it with certainty   Her allowance for the present month shall be sent in the course of two or three days   It will be necessary to add a servant to my present number, after Mrs Butler comes to reside here whose exclusive duty will be to attend upon her   If the person at present in Mrs Butler's employ is agreeable to her, I will engage her, or any other one she may prefer   Will you be good enough to ascertain this for me

"Yours, very sincerely,

"PIERCE BUTLER.

"Rev Mr Furness"   "<i>February</i> 6, 1845.

In the course of a few days I was enabled to write to Mr Furness again, and more definitively —

"Dear Sir,

"Mrs Butler's rooms will be ready for her on Monday, March 3d, on which day she can take up her residence in my house.

"Will you be so good as to obtain an answer to my inquiry respecting the woman now in her service

"Mrs Butler's allowance for the present month, has been sent to her, through the usual channel

"Yours, sincerely,

"PIERCE BUTLER.

"Rev. Mr Furness"   "<i>February</i> 19, 1845.

From the period of our practical disunion Mrs Butler had been paid her promised monthly allowance of two hundred and eight dollars, but of course the continuance of that amount, after she came to reside in my house, and thereby ceased to have any but mere personal expenses, while all of mine were necessarily much augmented, was entirely out of the question, I had, therefore apprized her through Mr Furness, that in future she would receive two hundred dollars a quarter In reference to this Mr Furness and I interchanged notes

‘ *February* 19, 1845

"Dear Sir,

"Mrs Butler wishes to keep her present maid servant She desires also to know what expenses her allowance ($800) is understood by you to be intended to cover, that is to say, is it merely for her clothes, or for all her personal and incidental expenses She likewise desires to be informed through whom she is to receive her allowance in future Will it not be well to have this all understood beforehand? And will you please to send me a word or two, as soon as may be, stating your understanding of these things?

‘ Your friend

W H Furness

"Pierce Butler, Esq"

" *Walnut Street*, 21 *February*, 1845

"Dear Sir,

"The sum of eight hundred dollars is intended to cover all Mrs Butler's personal and incidental expenses Before I fixed that sum, I made some inquiries which induce me to believe that no married lady in the city spends a like amount, taking one year with another I therefore deem it ample She shall receive the money directly from myself every month While Mrs Butler was living apart from me, on a separate maintenance, I did not consider her a member of my family, and therefore would hold no direct communication with her, when she comes to reside under my roof the case will be entirely altered, she will then be one of the family In order to protect myself and to insure domestic privacy, I have required that Mrs Butler shall not mention any circumstance which may occur in my

1

house or family, I shall myself, in the most careful manner, observe the same rule, and shall take care that it be observed by every person residing under my roof

"I require also, that Mrs. Butler shall not speak of me, neither will I mention her name to any one any communication that I may have to make to her, shall be made in writing, and shall be addressed to herself Under no circumstance will I allow the intervention of a third person in any matter between us, after she enters my family.

"In accordance with your suggestion, that it will be well to have every thing understood beforehand, I enclose a paper, which Mrs. Butler can copy and sign, she can then send me the one in her own handwriting, and keep the one now sent for her own reference I deem this necessary, for, although my letters have been perfectly explicit on the subject of Mrs. Butler's application to reside in my house, hers have not been so clear. the only letter from her, in which there is any intention expressed of complying with the required conditions, is far from being explicit, but, as I understood her to promise full compliance with the conditions I have named, she can have no hesitation in saying so, in language which does not admit of misinterpretation I have therefore written out the understood conditions, to which I must request her signature, in order to prevent as far as possible any future misunderstanding

"Yours, sincerely,

' PIERCE BUTLER

" Rev. Mr FURNISS "

The following is the paper alluded to, which was submitted for her signature —

"Being about to reside in Mr Butler's house, I promise to observe the following conditions while living under his roof —

"I will give up all acquaintance and intercourse of whatever kind, whether by word or letter with every member of the Sedgwick family, and hereafter I will treat them in every respect as entire strangers and as if I had never known them

' I will not keep up an acquaintance with any person, of whom Mr Butler may disapprove

" I will observe an entire abstinence from all reference to the past, neither will I mention to any person any circumstance which may occur in Mr Butler's house or family

' I will neither write nor speak of Mr Butler to any one while I remain under his roof I will also conform to the arrangements of his house, as I shall find them on entering it, and I promise, if I find myself unable to fulfil any of the aforesaid conditions, immediately to give notice to Mr Butler of my inability to do so, and to leave his house "

It will be seen that these terms are precisely those originally proposed through Mr Meredith and by which Mrs Butler had, with a clear comprehension of their scope and cause, pledged herself to abide I was, therefore, somewhat at a loss to conjecture her design and motive in withholding her signature, and in resorting to a frivolous quibble as an excuse

" *Monday, Feb* 24.

" My dear Sir,

" Will you oblige me by informing Mr Butler that as I have acceded to and am prepared to comply with the terms which he proposed to me through Mr Meredith, last May, and to which he refers in his letters to you (of which I presume he has a copy), as the *only* ones upon which he will permit me to live with my children, I must beg to decline signing any document or contract, which, if it contain new conditions, I cannot comply with and if it does not is unnecessary.

    " I am, my dear Sir

        " Yours, very truly,

                · FANNY BUTLER.

" REV MR FURNESS '

" Dear Sir,

" In my letter to you of the 21st instant, I stated a sufficient reason for wishing Mrs Butler to sign the conditions, it was, that her compliance with them had not been expressed in explicit language. It was partly in consequence of your own suggestion, that I drew out the conditions in simple form, for her to copy and sign In doing so, I inserted nothing new, on the contrary I copied the very words in which the conditions had been expressed Mrs Butler now refuses to sign them, for she will not comply with any new conditions, and she thinks it unnecessary to sign those, which she has already acceded to. To her, this may seem a sufficient reason for wishing to avoid a compliance in positive and unmistakable terms, for me it is not sufficient Mrs Butler has given me little reason to place any reliance upon either her good feelings, or her good faith towards me, and in admitting her into my house, I can perceive no security for myself against her violating, as heretofore, all the proprieties of domestic life, unless she is bound by positive terms, to which a consequence is attached Her letter has added strength to this opinion, for there is a plain design to observe only the words of the conditions, and not their spirit. I therefore require, before she comes here, that she shall copy and sign the paper I have sent.

    " Yours, sincerely,

        " PIERCE BUTLER.

        " *Walnut street, Feb. 25, 1845.*

" REV MR FURNESS "

Upon this Mrs Butler signed the paper, taking care, however, to preface it with a sort of precautionary protest —

"In order to remain near my children, and retain as far as possible the rights of a mother over them, I agreed fully and unconditionally, to certain terms which Mr Butler referred to, and insisted on, in a letter to Mr Furness, of December 13, 1844 Mr Butler now demands that I should copy and sign the following agreement, stating that he considers it to contain and signify nothing new or in any way different from the former one, with which understanding, I proceed to copy and sign it."

Accordingly she once more returned as a resident to my habitation on March 3, 1845

DESERTION.

I HAD made such careful and commodious arrangements for the accommodation of Mrs Butler, as almost persuaded me to hope that her stay would be
permanent and that thenceforward a becoming tranquillity at least would mark our unhappy relations
She had her own apartments, and her own servant we
met but once each day, at the dinner table with our
two children, and then none but unavoidable verbal
communications passed between us She was free to
come and go as she pleased, received visits at all hours
without my knowing or caring who made them, gave
social parties when she liked, and, in fact, I scrupulously forbore doing anything to re-excite discord or
engender trouble But her captious and uncontrolled
temper would neither rest itself, nor permit me to
rest her propensity to rebuke, to find fault, and to
exasperate her own discontent, soon rekindled I had
thought it most in the interest of domestic peace that
all our communications, except those at meals, should
take the form and formality of writing, and lo! there
was scarcely an occurrence or circumstance which
could possibly be worked up into a pretext for dissatis-

faction, that she did not with her usual tact and talent, spread forth in epistolary complaint A trivial incident, to which families with young children are daily liable formed the burden of an elaborate letter shortly after she entered the house As the nurse one morning was attending to the children, the younger of the two, happening to be out of humour, sulkily resisted being dressed, the nurse asked the governess whose room adjoined, to speak to her this, however, only increased the child's passion, and, becoming fractious, she struck the governess who then gave her a smart slap As I had strictly prohibited corporal punishment under any circumstances, the governess thought it necessary immediately to report the occurrence, stating that the slap was given as the only means of producing an impression and allaying her paroxysm of temper I repeated my injunction never again to do the like to either of the children, and to my certain knowledge this was the solitary occasion The next day Mrs Butler sent me the following —

"I am very desirous not to create any difficulties in the house, or interfere in any way with the arrangements you have seen fit to make. A circumstance occurred, however, yesterday morning which, after due deliberation, I think it best to inform you of I was waked in the morning by the screams of my youngest child and on going up to the nursery in some alarm found that she had conducted herself ill, and that Miss Hall had whipped her You may perhaps remember that only once did I ever lift a hand on either of the children, and then I told you my determination never to do so again You do not, I am very sure, resort to any such mode of enforcing your will, and I trust you will so far admit and uphold my right over my children, as not to permit, while I am under the same roof with them, that any one should adopt a mode of controlling them which neither I, nor, I presume, yourself, approve of, or ever have recourse to "

On getting this, I interrogated the nurse about the matter, and again spoke to the governess both assured me that but one slap had been inflicted This was magnified by Mrs Butler into a "whipping," and the inference invoked was that "the screams" which drew her to the nursery in "alarm" were produced by that rude treatment, whereas, in reality they were mere outbursts of childish vexation, to which the single slap put an end I answered her note thus —

"*March* 20, 1845

"The occurrence of yesterday morning had been correctly reported to me *I do not approve of striking children, and will not of course permit it with my own* It cannot, with any degree of correctness, be termed 'a whipping' that the child received, she refused to obey either the nurse or governess, and would not allow herself to be dressed, she was slapped once, which caused her to submit It shall not be repeated "

Soon came another murmuring missive · it required no answer, but contained one sentence liable to misconstruction, and which exacted a notice from me ·—

"*April* 10, 1845.

"There is a part of your letter which it is necessary to have explained You write thus—'a state of things which permits my children s governess to say that she will have *my maid* discharged.' I request to know upon whose authority you state this "

She replied —

" The children's nurse told Biddy about a week ago that Miss Hall had said to her, that she would have my maid discharged The latter informed me of this expressing at the same time her hope that she should not lose her situation, without in any way having deserved to do so "

Having made the proper scrutiny and satisfied myself that this assertion was untrue, I answered —

" *April* 11, 1845

" The nurse denies positively having said any such thing to Biddy as you report, and moreover says, that the governess never said to her that she would have your maid discharged, or any thing at all like it It would be well not to make the tales and tattle of servants the subject of your letters to me "

A casual circumstance, of which Mrs Butler makes much dexterous use in her ' *Narrative*,'' occurred about this time It will bear, I admit the ingenious construction she has placed upon it, but that construction is, nevertheless, neither true nor just It was this After she had rejoined the household a little over a month, there came enclosed to me a letter for her, which I at once saw by the exterior handwriting to be from a Sedgwick After all that had passed, any attempt to open a correspondence could be regarded no otherwise than as an impertinent intrusion , and entertaining no doubt but that Mrs Butler would view it in the same light would instantly appreciate the motive of delicacy which forbade my detaining what was addressed to her, would decline opening it,

U

and would either return it to me or send it back to the writer, I enclosed it to her without remark She did not do, however, as I had anticipated, but read and kept the letter whether she answered it or not, is unknown to me I did not wonder at an effort of the Sedgwicks to open a means of ascertaining the events of my household. that was in character but I felt real surprise that Mrs Butler, having bound herself so recently and explicitly to "give up all ac-"quaintance and intercourse of whatever kind, whether "by word or letter, with every member of the family," should, under any circumstances countenance that effort Irritated at what struck me to be in violation of a positive promise, and ignorant to what extent it would be carried, I wrote to her

"You have lived in this house a little over a month and you have already violated the principal condition which you bound yourself to observe, while living under my roof I will hold no intercourse with a person so utterly wanting in truth and good faith and therefore request you to address no more notes to me

"*April 12th, 1845*"

To which she replied —

"I have not the least understanding of what you mean If you refer to the letter which I received through your intermission yesterday, all I can say is that I was as much surprised as you could possibly be at the circumstance of its being sent hither, and I opened it only because enclosed to me by you, which otherwise I should certainly not have done

"If this is *not* what you refer to I know not what you mean, and utterly deny the charge of having broken any part of the bond you made me sign."

I answered thus —

"Before you came into this house you should have informed the
Sedgwicks of the conditions to which you had bound yourself, and
warned them to write to you no more it is probable that you did so,
but being vulgar and obtrusive people, they are attempting to persevere in their officious meddling in my domestic concerns You
were bound by your obligation to return unread and in a blank cover,
any letter which you knew to come from them

"Your doing so by their first letter, might prevent a repetition of
such indelicate conduct, and save my house from being infested by
their correspondence Your not doing so is a direct encouragement
to them to persevere and your reading and detaining their letter, is
a violation of all truth and honour on your part

"*April 12th*, 1845 "

Of this transaction she says, ' As one of the clauses
' of my contract of sojourn was, that I should forego
all intercourse with every member of this family, I
' was much surprised at receiving this enclosure from
· the libellant but I supposed he had some special
" motive for sending it to me, and as we exchanged no
" communication other than written, this appeared to
'· me to indicate that he chose me to receive the let-
" ter, and I accordingly opened and read it I im-
" mediately, however perceived my mistake on re-
' ceiving the following note from the libellant ' She
then inserts my first note of April 12 and adds, " I
felt myself completely caught in a trap ×
I willingly concede that she acted under the impression alleged by herself, that · she supposed I had

"some special motive for sending the letter to her," that my doing so ' appeared to her to indicate that I "chose her to receive it," and on reflection I acquit her in this instance of that breach of truth and honour which I hastily imputed Nothing however, can be more absurd or unfounded than to predicate of the mere forbearance to detain or destroy the letter, any design on my part to set "a trap" Both of us acted under misapprehension of motives and when I wrote those two notes it had not occurred to me, as is now apparent, that my enclosing and sending the letter to her might readily be thought to involve my consent to her receiving it

Notwithstanding all the precautions I had taken the privacy of my household continued in some way or other, and by the agency of some one, subject to the surveillance and animadversion of others Nothing could shelter it from the perseverance of curiosity or the perversion of scandal Who it was that took pleasure in this meddlesome and miserable pursuit I am unwilling to conjecture but certain it is that I received letters from friends of Mrs Butler in England, which proved how futile my arrangements had been, and how liable as ever to distortion and slander were the simplest features of my domestic life A portion of my own part in this correspondence will serve to exhibit this petty and dishonourable warfare upon my peace The first letter is to a lady a friend of Mrs Butler and also, as I believed, a friend of mine

"*Philadelphia, June* 29, 1845.

"My dear Mrs Mackintosh

"There are two reasons which will prevent me from taking offence at your last two letters, first because I cannot suppose you intended to offend me, and also because I think you cannot be sensible of the extraordinary manner in which you have written to me   I write to you now that you may know your letters have been received, to answer them is impossible, for I do not understand them. Who have been troubling themselves to write to you about my domestic affairs, I know not neither can I tell, from the tenor of your letter, what they have written   that falsehood has been written is evident   Does it never occur to you that it is somewhat unwise and useless, for a third person to attempt to regulate the affairs of a husband and wife, who do not agree together?   And does it not strike you that no person can be very capable of regulating the details of another's family at a distance of three thousand miles?   You have no doubt relied upon the information you received, but it would have been well first to ascertain if it were correct, coming as it must from some person not a member of my family   You accuse me of unfair dealing and want of confidence and openness   you say that I constrain Fanny, and do not give her the life of a gentlewoman, and that I make her position in my house that of an inferior, you tell me to give her her meals in her own room, and to discharge the governess of my children   This last act you charge me to perform for my children's sake, and for my own comfort and respectability, and you entreat me, if I have any wish that Fanny should remain in my house to take some measures for appointing a successor to Miss Hall   You consider her presence an insult to Fanny, and you do not believe that our present life can, or ought to go on while she remains   If you believe all you have charged against me, I wonder you would write to me   if it be true, it is proof that I have laid aside the character and feelings of a gentleman, and it becomes a question if those qualities ever belonged to me   Why have you written to me? Can you hope to influence the conduct of a man who seeks to degrade the mother of his children in the eyes of those children? And will you hold intercourse of any sort with one who admits his wife into his house only for the purpose of insulting her? Can there be one good feeling left to such a man which you hope to act upon? All these things you deliberately charge against me, and I find it not very pleasant to learn the estimation in which you hold me. To whom I am indebted for painting my character in such colours, I am at a loss to conceive, the conception is worthy the mind of a Sedgwick

"As I do not know what has been written to you I cannot answer your objections as to the governess. If you will tell me exactly what has been told you—and I think you are bound to do so—I will reply to you. But why should she not continue with the children? And how is her presence an insult to Fanny? What is her offence? I presume that some kind friend of mine has given you the information upon which you found your charges, but until you communicate it to me I am unable to reply

"Believe me,

"Very sincerely, your friend,

"PIERCE BUTLER"

The following went at the same time to Mrs Sartoris, the sister of Mrs Butler —

"*Philadelphia, June* 29, 1845.

"My dear Adelaide,

"Your last letter is quite incomprehensible to me, and I am unable to reply to it. It is not of the most agreeable character, but as you assure me that you write in the spirit of real friendship, I send this acknowledgment of its receipt. It was well you put in that assurance, else I should have supposed you wrote in quite a different spirit. Here are some of the things you say:—' Let me entreat you

'to modify that most unjust and intolerable arrangement by which
'Miss Hall (a *hired* instructress) supersedes my sister in her right
'and control over her children. *No woman would bear such an in-*
'*tolerable* insult as this. From the moment my sister returned to
'take her proper place Miss Hall ought to have been dismissed at
'once.' 'I must say that this' &c. &c.

"'I beseech you to alter this dreadful state of things as much for
'your and your children's sakes as for that of my sister.'

'These are some of the pleasant things you say. I quote them
because you may have forgotten the tenor of your letter, as you say
you were greatly hurried when you wrote. When Fanny came to
live here I thought and hoped I was to have something like peace in
my family, and domestic privacy. Which of my kind friends has
given you the reliable information upon which you found these
charges I do not know, nor do I know what has been told you.
However if you will tell me—as you are bound to do—what you
have heard, and from whom it comes, I will reply to it. I will also
tell you whether it is true, or not, which point you do not appear to
have given yourself the trouble to ascertain. There has been such
a shameful system of falsehood carried on with regard to my affairs,
that it is really unendurable. Vague insinuations I cannot reply to,
but only let me know distinctly what you have heard, and I will answer you truly and fully.

"Yours ever affectionately,

"PIERCE BUTLER."

Both ladies replied to my letters, but neither of
them told me from whom had proceeded the vile calumnies which obviously impelled their remonstrances.

Intolerable as was this subjection to a system of
espionage, to having the whole tenor of my life falsified, and to be actually taken to task concerning the

routine of my household, I was further chafed by an occurrence somewhat more grave and unpleasant The following note, addressed to me by the governess of my children, will explain it —

"Dear Sir,

"In a letter received yesterday, from my sister, the following passage occurs, which I consider it my painful duty to lay before you, requesting you to take such steps as you deem best to make the author of the report deny what she has said, or explain her reasons for saying what is reported

" Mrs Carpenter while in London, heard from her son, Dr.
' Carpenter, what I think it best to tell you, painful as it is, namely,
' Mrs Butler s scandalous reports respecting yourself, that a crimi-
' nal connexion between her husband and you was the cause of her
' leaving him, &c &c &c Lady Byron and Lady Lovelace men-
' tioned this to Dr Carpenter who said the thing was impossible,
' speaking of the high respectability of our family, but expressed
' surprise to his mother that you remained under the circumstances.
' She, fortunately, had heard all your letters, and could answer him
' fully, saying, you remained contrary to the wishes of your friends
' here, but out of consideration to the children, and at the earnest
' desire of Mr Butler's family and most respectable relatives.
' The whole of Mrs Butler s statement being a tissue of falsehood,
' you perhaps may not be surprised at anything she utters, however
' base or black '

" Thus ends the paragraph, and I am not surprised, but, knowing it, consider it a duty to my character that the subject should be in-vestigated, and that Mrs Butler should explicitly, and in writing, either deny what she has said, or state her motives for propagating such a falsehood.

" In your hands I leave it, and believe me, &c.

" AMELIA HALL

" *June 22, 1845* "

An appeal thus frankly and directly made to my sense of justice and of honour, could be treated in one decisive way only. I felt bound, by every consideration to trace, if possible, so scandalous a report to its source, and to demand its unqualified recantation. In requiring a distinct disclaimer from Mrs Butler, I fully explained by extracts from the letters of her friends in England, and also from the foregoing note my grounds for doing so. The communication addressed to her respecting this heartless and baseless calumny, however explicit, is as I conceive, worded temperately under the circumstances, and would, by conscious innocence, have been answered with equal promptness and positiveness.

' *June* 28, 1843.

" A short time ago I received letters from Mrs Sartoris and Mrs Mackintosh, both of whom are your correspondents. These letters were incomprehensible to me, and contained expressions which I did not understand. Mrs. Mackintosh says, I entreat you, if you ' have any wish (either for your children's sake, your own comfort ' or respectability) that Fanny should remain in your house—to take ' some measures for appointing a successor to Miss Hall. I must ' consider her presence an insult to Fanny and I do not believe your ' present life can or ought to go on while she remains. Mrs Sartoris says, Let me entreat you to modify that most unjust and in- ' tolerable arrangement by which Miss Hall (a *hired* instructress) ' supersedes my sister in her right and control over her children, ' *No* woman would bear such an *intolerable* insult as this.' There ' is but one opinion about it here, and that is, that from the moment ' my sister returned to take her proper place, Miss Hall ought to ' have been dismissed at once. All your and our friends are in the

X

'extremest surprise that this should not have been arranged by you
'previous to Fanny's return to your house'

"All this was perfectly inexplicable to me, for I did not know who
or what had induced these two ladies to write to me in this manner
and I was totally at a loss to understand why Miss Hall should not
remain as the governess of my children, still more was I at a loss
to conceive how her presence could be an insult to you It seemed
strange, indeed, that while I considered her a proper person to in-
struct my children, that persons living in England should undertake
to rule my domestic arrangements, and should urge me to dismiss
her, nor could I interpret the grave insinuations which their expressions seemed to convey Some light has been cast upon the subject
by a letter which Miss Hall herself has just received from her sister
in England, an extract from which has been communicated to me,
it is as follows 'Mrs Carpenter, while in London, heard from her
'son, Dr Carpenter, what I think it best to tell you, painful as it is,
'namely, Mrs Butler's scandalous reports respecting yourself, that
'a criminal connexion between her husband and you was the cause
'of her leaving him, &c &c &c Lady Byron and Lady Lovelace
'mentioned this to Dr Carpenter'

"This report is stated to come from Lady Byron and Lady Lovelace, it is probable that Mrs Jameson was their informant, she has
constant intercourse with them, and she is a correspondent of yours
It is necessary that you should say whether or not you have originated such a report, or whether you have ever said any thing which
could give rise to it I require your answer to be plain and direct,
so as either to confirm you as the author, or to disprove it totally

"PIERCE BUTLER."

I expected this matter, so serious in its import, and
which no light-minded or true-hearted woman could
possibly treat with levity, would receive immediate
attention Two entire days, however, were allowed

to elapse and even then no direct disclaimer or ex-
culpation was attempted, but I was sent a frivolous
and evasive reply, ending with the cold-blooded insi-
nuation that she was "not at all surprised" at the
disadvantageous reports about one of her own sex
whose innocence she perfectly knew.

"*June* 30.

* * * "As for the letter I received from you on Saturday, I
have been really at a loss how to reply to it—to an accusation of
spreading scandalous reports brought against me by an utter stranger, I have of course no answer to make, with the contents of the
letters of your English correspondents I have nothing to do, still less
with those of Miss Hall which she communicated to you   If my
sister or Mrs. Mackintosh write to you about your affairs, it is neither at my instigation, nor with my knowledge   I am sorry for the
disadvantageous reports in circulation about Miss Hall, but not at all
surprised at them, as they are the natural and inevitable consequence
of her position in your family for the past year."

Such an answer irresistibly forced upon my mind,
after what had passed, the conviction that Mrs Butler had been, at least, an accessary to these cruel and
debasing reports, and under the influence of indignant and outraged feeling, I immediately again wrote

'*July* 1, 1845.

"It is impossible to make any impression on one whose mental
and moral obliquity blinds her to all the vices of her nature, whose
reason is sophistry, whose religion is cant, and whose unbounded
self-esteem renders her happy and satisfied in all her wrong doings
therefore I have no hope that you will ever comprehend, much less
fulfil, your duty as a mother   In the endeavour to discharge my

duty to my children, I am as much bound to protect those who have
in any way the care of them, and who are sheltered by my roof as
I am bound to protect my children themselves. An infamous scandal having been reported concerning their instructress, it is but right
that it should be denied and disproved, and this for their sakes as
much as for hers. Therefore I again require, that you will explicitly state whether or not, you have ever said anything against the
character of Miss Hall or anything which could originate the report
alluded to. Your having refused an answer gives me the strongest
impression that you have done so, and if you do not fear to speak
the truth, why not answer explicitly a simple question? You ought
to perceive that such a report is, in reality, more injurious to your
children than even to Miss Hall herself and, unless disproved, it
places you in a most discreditable position, for consenting to sit at
table, day after day, with such a character. Deny, therefore, if you
can, having originated the infamous calumny, and clear yourself from
an imputation that the vilest woman would be ashamed of."

To which she rejoined —

"*Wednesday, July 2*

"You appear to overlook the fact, that in bringing an accusation
of defamation against me, you are bound to prove it otherwise than
by your suspicions or the affirmation of a person who is a stranger
to me, and as the guilt of propagating malignant falsehoods is, in
my opinion, greater than that of a breach of chastity, I beg you will
do so. You have also forgotten that the mere simple denial of a
person accused (and by yourself, as you state, strongly suspected)
of what you charge me with, would be utterly worthless, as any-
body, capable of one lie, would hardly scruple to shield himself by
another. The intemperate tone of your letter makes those inconsis-
tencies less surprising than they would otherwise be, and I will only

add, that I protest most solemnly against the unworthy treatment to which I am subjected, and which I have in no way deserved."

Mrs Butler, in her "*Narrative*," filed in Court, says —"At the same time I addressed a note to the 'governess, denying that I had ever spoken, written, 'or even *thought* the injurious things respecting her, "which were attributed to me"* This note was not shown to myself nor was I aware of its existence until some days after its date and delivery Had a copy of it been communicated to me, or a frank and direct answer to my explicit interrogatory, Mrs Butler would have been spared the letter of July 1st, which she extorted only by her perverse preference of adroit trifling to ingenuous truth She affirms that she never "even *thought*" anything against the governess It is, then, much to be regretted that she so frequently suggested the imminent danger of injurious reports, as nothing so certainly or more artfully gives birth to a calumny than a constant allusion to the likelihood of its rise To entertain such delicate matters as probabilities precedes but little their being treated as certainties, and scandal hinted soon blooms into scandal asserted It is the invariable sequence She knew Miss Hall too well to be audacious enough to assail her directly, but, nevertheless, she often declared that remaining in my family would end in the loss of her reputation She reiterates this several times in her "*Narrative*," and here are two occasions, out of many — ·The resi- "dence of the governess in his house, under all the "circumstances through which she had persisted in it,

"had not escaped observation and comment, and, as I
"had fully anticipated had led to the most disadvan-
"tageous and painful rumours with regard to her cha-
"racter '* Again — I am sorry for the disadvan-
"tageous reports in circulation about Miss Hall, but
"not at all surprised at them "† That she habitually maintained this tone, I know, and the frequency
with which, in her " *Narrative*," she thrusts forward
the name of the governess, betrays to the most casual
observer an eagerness to fortify those rumours which
she dared not openly countenance, but which she had
" fully anticipated," and " was not at all surprised at "
There can be no reasonable doubt, I have never entertained the slightest, that these atrocious slanders
had no other source or origin than Mrs Butler's own
light and loose language

It is, perhaps, but just, and may not be out of place
here, to introduce a letter from myself to Mr Hall,
written at the time his sister relinquished the care of
my children and returned to her own country and
kindred The high estimation expressed of that lady
was common to every member of my family, and, in
fact to all who knew her

" *Philadelphia, Nov. 4, 1845.*

" My dear Sir,

" Your sister having fully determined to leave us, I cannot allow
her to go without writing to you to express my very great regret at
her departure. Her going is altogether her own act, and glad should
I be, if she could have been content to remain So well satisfied have
I been with her care and management of my children for three years
that I have had no wish with regard to them, but that she should re-

---

main their instructress until they were grown up. Mild, judicious, and untiring in her attention to their studies, they have made a rapid advance in knowledge, and their minds have developed steadily and healthily. It is not only in the school room, and as an instructress, that I place so high an estimate on Miss Hall's qualities, I looked to my children's deriving as much benefit from their companionship with her, as from anything else. Her gentleness, amiability, and kindness have strongly attached them to her, and I believe their dispositions would naturally have taken their character from hers. My children will be great losers by Miss Hall's departure, for there is no hope of finding any lady to fill her place. Your sister carries with her the respect and esteem of every member of my family, and their regret at her loss to us is equal with mine. They, as well as myself, will always feel an interest in her welfare, and will ever remember with kind feelings her excellent care of my children.

    " I remain, my dear sir,

       ' Yours, very truly

          " PIERCE BUTLER

" JOHN ROBERT HALL, Esq. *London* "

From the moment Mrs. Butler rejoined the family so far from endeavouring to 'conform to the arrangements of my house as she found them on entering it," agreeably to her written pledge, she exhibited an uncurbed anxiety to bring about occasions of controversy and disturbance, and fan into flame every little latent spark of strife. To myself she allowed no repose. I was called upon by her rapid epistles to remodel almost every department of the domestic administration. She repelled quiet and courted contention. Under such influences it was also natural she should not get on smoothly with the children. Unceasing war against their father was not likely to

maintain peace with them   Absence for more than a
year had weakened her maternal authority, and her
course after return was ill calculated to re-establish it
Angry differences arose between them, which she attributed to various causes, but never the true one,
nor would she permit herself to perceive that having
failed in the duty of a wife she necessarily lost her
rightful position as a mother   On the happening of
a most painful and violent altercation with her elder
daughter, she led her by the arm to me that I might
enforce the child's submission   Mrs Butler was in a
glare of excitement, and I did not reply to her, but
told the child she must be obedient   Deprecating the
baneful effects upon my daughter's character consequent upon such scenes I determined, if possible to
arrest them   The subjoined letter to Mrs Butler
illustrates partially the wretched discord that reigned

" *June* 29, 1845

" I must request that you will have nothing to say, or to do with
Sarah   This is absolutely necessary for the child's welfare. The
contentions between you must cease, for their effect upon her character and disposition will be dreadful   It is not in my power to
control her behaviour to you, it is the reward you are reaping for
your own past misconduct   The total loss of affection, duty, and
obedience which she shows for you, is the result of your own violation of all the duties of a wife and a mother   Had you been true to
your obligations to your children, you would not now suffer the humiliation of their loss of respect for you   A mother who abandons
her children, cannot expect to have the same hold upon their affections, when she returns to them, after a desertion of more than one
year   Sarah's quick perceptions have enabled her to form her own
opinions, she has judged you, and condemns you   You have lost

all influence over her, and your appeals to me to make her treat you with respect are utterly vain, it is not in my power, nor in that of any human being, to restore that which your own conduct has forfeited The authority of a parent once abandoned and broken up, cannot easily be regained or repaired Your position, such as it is, was made and is maintained by yourself You abandoned your children, you vilified their father, you defamed those who were about them, and who by kindness had gained their affection, you created discord and dissension in my home, you broke up and destroyed every vestige of domestic peace and happiness, and you exposed and made public the unhappy state of our family affairs You regarded neither truth, honour, nor decency in your assaults upon me, you scrupled at nothing, you stopped at nothing, in your endeavour to dishonour and discredit me in the world's opinion You made my bitter enemies your chosen friends, you hunted me yourself, and you set them on to hunt me too. You separated yourself from me, and your dearest object would have been gained, could you have succeeded in depriving me of all control over my children You took no pains to conceal your conduct from the children, you let them know what you were about, and you set the eldest child, if indeed not both of them, to think for herself She did think, and now you wonder that she does not consider you with respect Nothing that I can do, nothing that any one can do will efface from Sarah's mind the effects of your conduct. You must at once cease all communication with her, you cast away a mother's rightful claim over your child, and you cannot recover it Her will is strong, and she can only be ruled by kindness and affection, these are influences which you can no longer exert over her You have rendered my home wretched and miserable, and it will gratify you to know that you have completely destroyed my happiness in life Forbear, for God's sake, and do not destroy the happiness of your child With the younger child, you have still some influence left, exert it as

Y

beneficially as you may. With Sarah, you can do nothing but harm, you have roused her strong spirit of resistance to injustice, and you cannot master it, for God's sake, let her alone."

An additional illustration of the distraction and turmoil which Mrs Butler so sedulously fomented, may be found in her account of the visit of the children to the country in the summer of that year—1845 She has represented this with such elaborate and preposterous distortion as to make it appear an injury to my daughters, and a wrong to herself, that they were sent out of town in the dog-days The illness of my father and of another near relative confined me to the city, but the children could not be allowed to remain, and the best retreat for them, as appeared to me, was a farm of my own in a salubrious and retired spot only six miles off I arranged for their temporary accommodation at that place, as one easily accessible, and I felt sure of both their safety and happiness while there This simple and satisfactory measure for their health and welfare was, like most others, assailed by Mrs Butler, and instantly seized as another theme for her prolific pen —

" I hope you will be good enough to make such arrangements as will not separate my children from me. I came to your house to be with them, and have a right to expect that they will not be placed where I cannot be with them.

"*July 14th* "

I replied to her objection —

" I have made an arrangement to send the children to the Darby farm for two or three weeks, with their former nurse, Ann Martin, the only servant who was ever able to exercise any control over them, and under whose care they will be perfectly safe I would not send them to a public watering-place, unless I accompany them myself, which I am unable to do, on account of the illness of my father and aunt

" *Tuesday, July 15th.*"

Accordingly they went to the Darby farm I usually visited them twice a week Mrs Butler was at perfect liberty to visit them whenever she pleased nor could she possibly find it inconvenient to do so, as she was in the habit of taking daily and long rides on horseback for her own recreation

The only dwelling on this farm was occupied by the farmer and his family, who could spare but one room, and that, indeed, was all-sufficient for the two children and their nurse But Mrs Butler was inflexibly bent on frustrating the plan, or failing in that, to convert it into a pretext for final desertion The children were no sooner gone than she issued another despatch —

" The circumstances under which I obtained admission to the home of my children certainly entitled me to expect that they would not again be removed from me I must, therefore, once more request that you will not persist in separating them from me Fanny was very unwell when she left town, and I cannot consent to be prevented from seeing my child under such circumstances The accommodation which is sufficient for the person who is now with them is quite sufficient for me, and I am at least as competent as any hired attendant to the care of my own children * * *

" *July 17th* "

To which I answered —

"The children have been sent out of town for their benefit, they cannot be better off than they are at present   You are not refused access to them, you can go to visit them in your rides, and can see them as often as I do myself   There is no room for another person in the house with them, nor is it necessary that any one else should be with them for the time they are to remain there   I saw them yesterday, and left them both quite well   *   *   *

"*July* 18*th*, 1845."

Although the excessive inconvenience, if not the impossibility, of her residing in the house with the children, owing to actual want of room, was apparent and known to Mrs Butler, she was, nevertheless, pertinacious, and addressed me still another note, in which she says —

*   *   *   *   "I again reiterate my request to be admitted to the house where my children are living, as a separation of this sort from them was of course not what I contemplated when I came hither solely for the purpose of being with them

"*July* 19*th*."

This miserable doggedness of temper which sought on all occasions to weary me into surrendering my arrangements and views to her own, and which had been practised with little intermission since her abode under my roof, wrung from me a reply which I idly hoped might relieve me from its continuance —

*   *   *   *   "The pretence of not being able to bear a short separation from your children, while they are enjoying themselves

in the country is hollow and absurd   You wilfully abandoned them
for fourteen months without a struggle and only this week you went
away from them for four days, leaving the younger child much in-
disposed   They shall remain where they are, and as they are, until
I think proper to bring them back to the city

"*July 19th.*"

She now undertook to act in defiance of my distinctly communicated determination and wishes, she
went to the farm she turned the nurse out of her
bed—the only one there was for her—and coolly assumed possession for herself   Such conduct was
flagrant, and obliged me to repeat what I had done
on the performance of a similar feat of rebellion,
when, by her wilful misconduct she so nearly brought
serious consequences upon herself and me at the Yellow Springs *   I accordingly drove to the farm and
brought the children away

Her version of this last proceeding is given with
dramatic talent and effect —

' I accordingly went to the farm, and prepared to
" make it my residence as long as my children should
" remain there   After tea I suddenly heard that the
" libellant had arrived, the children went out to meet
" him, and I remained alone working by the waning
" daylight   Presently the libellant burst into my
" room, and drawing the door after him which opened
" between the farmer's room and the one where I was
" sitting, he said, in an under tone, but with the most
" furious manner —'I told you not to come here,—
" 'now you or the children leave this place to-night

* See page 94

" ' I'll have no words with you !' after which he rushed
" out of the other door, and so left me "*

Having " rushed out of the other door" I waited a
short time for some manifestation of her purpose.
She was immovable I therefore directed the nurse
to equip the children, and " in spite of the damp night
" air, for it had rained all the afternoon,—in spite of
" the gathering darkness, for it was past eight o'clock
" and thick twilight, the libellant persisted in taking
" away the two poor children, who departed crying,
" without bidding me good-by, or even seeing me
" again ' †

The next morning she came into town The
weather was oppressively warm My daughters necessarily suffered greatly Their mother had interrupted
the enjoyments of their rural retreat, and rendered
their stay at the farm impossible But I am never
discouraged when their good is in view, and in the
course of a couple of days proceeded to search within
a range of a few miles for suitable lodgings I was
not successful, and returned the same afternoon On
reaching home I learned that Mrs Butler had again
gone to the Darby farm with the children, " where,"
she says, " they were delighted to get back "‡ She
left them there and came home, " having made up her
mind not to return to the farm "§

Among the means of harassing within the power of
Mrs Butler was that of withholding her signature to
conveyances or deeds relating to real estate, and thus

---

* Mrs. Butler's *Narrative*," p 21   † Idem, p 22

‡ Idem, p 22.   § Idem, p 22

hindering transactions of business An instance of this sort occurred a person desired to pay off a ground rent upon his property and was entitled to a deed of release or extinguishment the document—perfectly simple in its import—was prepared and sent to her with the following note —

"Your signature is required to the accompanying deed It is the extinguishment of a ground rent, as you will see by looking at it

"*August 8th*, 1845 "

She refused to sign, and thus placed me in a position at once awkward and vexatious, unable to render to another the complete muniment which he had a perfect right to demand For such peevish obstinacy there seemed no remedy, I was without relief, and powerless I could hope for no effect from a retaliatory intimation, but as nothing else was possible, I addressed her as follows —

"Since you choose to thwart me in the management of my business, I give you notice that your allowance is discontinued, and I forbid you going to my farm where the children are.

"*August 8th*."

Previous to this, however, her allowance for that month—August—had been advanced, and as respects the prohibition upon her visits to the farm, she manifested for it her customary deference by going there the very same day

Mrs Butler anxiously struggles to evade the condemnation and shame of having wilfully deserted her husband and children, and her "*Narrative*" exhausts her stores of art, ingenuity, perversion and pretence, in efforts to persuade that she was actually driven from the sphere of her conjugal and parental duties She charges "not only cruelty on the part of the li- "bellant, but also his unlawful design to force me "from his habitation "* To inspire and sustain this belief, she has interwoven throughout numerous threads of untruth with such dexterity that to unravel the web, so as to separate what is false from what is fact, would be an almost endless undertaking Many of these strokes of deceit have already been dissected and refuted some others may not improperly be noticed She says, "The children having been sent to "the Darby farm, and the governess to a watering- "place, the house was given up to workmen to be "plastered and painted The libellant took up his "abode in his brother s house, and I remained alone "at the end of July, in the midst of dirt, confusion, "noise and discomfort of a house under repairs' †

Now in this single and short quotation are to be detected no less than four false suggestions And, first, "the governess having been sent to a watering- "place" A lady who had evinced a friendly feeling towards Miss Hall invited her to accompany herself and family to the Yellow Springs, she availed herself of the kindness and went, returning, however, before my children came back to the city, she was cordially welcomed to the house of one of my relatives, and there remained until her pupils were again at home and ready to resume their lessons It is,

* Mrs Butler's "*Narrative*," p 23   † Idem, p 20

therefore, not true that the governess was "sent" anywhere, and especially by me Second, 'the house 'was given up to workmen to be plastered and paint-"ed' No work was done in the house, other than painting the entries, patches of "dirt" may have been produced by washing and otherwise preparing the walls to receive the paint a process which occupied some three or four days, that being accomplished there was not even 'dirt" to offend the eye The painting was limited exclusively to the entries, not a room of the house was touched, and no 'plastering" at all attempted It is, therefore, not true that "the "house was given up to workmen to be plastered and "painted' Third ∙ The libellant took up his abode "in his brother s house " In my preparations for Mrs Butler s return and residence, I had assigned to her occupation and comfort the very best rooms the other good ones, those on the third floor, were appropriated to my daughters, their governess and the nurse For myself I had reserved an apartment in the back build-ings which proved in the summer so insufferably hot as to make the night sleepless, and I was induced to seek a cooler chamber at my brother's, immediately opposite, crossing the street only at night and only to sleep, for in every other particular my ∙ abode re-mained unaltered It is, therefore, not true that any 'repairs' to my own led me to "take up my abode 'in my brother's house" Fourth I remained "alone at the end of July, in the midst of dirt, con-"fusion, noise, and discomfort of a house under re-"pairs ' This description is equally fanciful unless the mere painting of an entry be construed into "a "house under repairs Much more plausibly might

z

every wife and mother, on the recurrence of the semi-annual period of house-cleaning, proclaim the hardship of witnessing domestic renovations, and so affect to be driven into the streets by the removal of carpets, scrubbing, and whitewashing

Among the countless trivialities and immaterialities of the "*Narrative,*' I must not be supposed intentionally to pass over, as incapable of contradiction, that which refers to some anonymous letters alleged to have been received by her

"Among the annoyances of that time, I do not "think it too unimportant to state that anonymous "letters were sent to me, copies of two whereof, ' marked Exhibits 10 A and 10 B, 1 annex, and "which, I was distressed to believe, were written by "the libellant, proof whereof, if desired, I crave leave "to adduce ' *

I feel much more authorized to assert that Mrs Butler wrote or caused to be written, these letters to herself, for the very purpose to which they are here put, than she could possibly find grounds for attributing them to me I do not think she ever sincerely believed them to be mine In reply to this unworthy charge, I can do no more than affirm myself to be incapable of so cowardly and mean a device that I neither wrote nor instigated the letters to which she refers, nor ever heard or knew of their existence until their production by her

Another wanton misstatement, very easily and conclusively disproved, is the following —

* Mrs Butler's ' *Narrative* p 13

"I was also often exceedingly inconvenienced by "the withholding of the allowance which the libellant ' made me as it was paid with great irregularity "*

It will be remembered that when she left me, in October, 1843, while we were yet at lodgings after our return from England, I voluntarily offered to let her have $2500 a year, to be paid monthly I continued this allowance uninterruptedly from that time to March, 1845, and she alludes to the instalments of that annual sum of $2500 when she ventures, under oath, to declare them to have been 'often withheld," and "paid with great irregularity ' I heard more than once that Mrs Butler had kindled against me the wrath of her companions by complaints as to the insufficiency of the sum I paid her, taking special care, however, never to state its amount, but further telling them that she obtained it from me with much difficulty The foregoing paragraph of her sworn 'Narrative is therefore, in strict accordance with her conversational representations I have it in my power, and with the undeniable attestations of her own receipting signatures, to show the entire absence of truth in her allegations as to "withholding" or "irregularity ' of payments With this view I annex the dates of those payments, made to her through her counsel, by whom her receipts were duly sent to me It will be seen that they were always in advance

1843	November 21,	1st payment, for	December,	$208
1844	January 2,	2d ,,	January,	208
,,	February 2.	3d ,,	February,	208
,,	March 1,	4th ,,	March,	208
,,	April 5,	5th ,,	April,	208

Mrs Butler's Narrative, p 8

1844. May 11,	6th payment, for May,			$208
„ June 18,	7th	„	June and July,	416
„ August 1,	8th	„	August,	208
„ September 7,	9th	„	September,	208
„ October 25,	10th	„	October and Nov	416
„ December 2,	11th	„	December,	$138
	Paid bill on her account,			70
				—— 208
1845. January 2,	12th payment for January,			208
„ February 19,	13th	„	February,	208

When, in March, 1845, Mrs Butler resumed her place as a member of my family, in my habitation, and was subject to no expenses other than merely personal ones, the allowance of $2500 ceased of course, and I named $800 as adequate to her then comparatively trifling wants   Many would deem this ample others, perhaps, insufficient   Let it be remembered that I could scarcely pretend, without hypocrisy, to any particular liberality towards one who, though still my wife, was an avowed enemy and open traducer So long as we had lived together on different terms, though discontented and dissatisfied always, she never had cause to reproach me, and she never did reproach me, with restricting her means, either for pleasures or necessities   What I possessed was as freely used by her as by myself   From March to September, 1845, six months, she was entitled to and obtained $400, but she did not scrupulously keep within the limits prescribed, soon after her departure, debts contracted by her to the amount of $450 were presented to me and paid   For the half year, therefore, preceding her final flight, she had more than doubled the stipulated allowance.

Mrs Butler had come into my house with reluctance and in truth much against her own will submitting to the pressure of the opinions and advice of her friends, who could no longer countenance or excuse her selfish and passionate estrangement from her children From the moment she crossed the threshold, she assiduously prepared to retrace her step This design was so apparent as to make manifestly useless, and far too vexatious and burdensome, the task of answering her almost daily communications After my brief note of August 8th I wrote no more Her letters to me, however, still flowed on

Disregarding her solemn engagements not to 'mention to any person any circumstance which may occur in Mr Butler's house or family,' and that she would "neither write nor speak of Mr Butler to any "one while I remain under his roof,'* she did write exactly as she pleased of every thing that took place This in her zeal to extenuate her conduct, she confesses —" My friends and family in England, whose ' advice I now demanded, strongly urged me for my "children's sake to come away, and I perceived the "necessity that I should do so † They whom she thus vouches as counsellors could know nothing of the condition of my domestic affairs except from the discoloured delineations of her pen nor was it easy for them, in view of her ever active and ever eloquent desire to be in England, to forbear encouraging what was so obviously in accordance with her own wishes, and what they probably foresaw she would do at every hazard

---

The children were to return to town early in September, and thus would then cease one of her subjects of complaint Their absence, no matter how meritorious its object, constituted her best pretext for the desertion and she could not wait even a few days, without risking the loss of that pretext Hence the following letter —

" The removal of my children for a couple of months from the house into which I was admitted upon conditions which I embraced SOLELY for the purpose of being with them, has of course cancelled those conditions I no longer feel myself in any way bound to observe them, for the sole purpose for which I undertook to do so has been defeated, and my children have been separated from me again, in spite of all my sacrifices to remain near them This compact being as far as I am concerned at an end, I now write to you under the expectation that my children must soon return home, once more to entreat you to reconsider the arrangements in your house and family, and to reorganize them in a manner which shall place me in my right relation towards my children, and them in their proper relation to me The experiment of the last six months must, I should think, have sufficed to show you that nothing but discomfort, disorder, and the most serious disadvantages could spring from the state of things which has existed in your house during that period The injury to the children has been terrible, and as that should be with you the most important of all considerations, I entreat and hope that for their sakes you will establish your household upon a footing that will obviate results which you must deplore as much as I do I have no desire to enter into any detail upon these painful subjects. In spite of your frequent absence from your house, you must have perceived what has escaped no one in it, the deplorable effects of the arrangements which have hitherto subsisted in it, and I again appeal to you for your own sake, for that of the children, and for justice sake.

to re-establish me in my rights and position as a mother, for which alone I came hither under the conditions which you imposed upon me, for which alone I am here still and which I trust you will yet be induced to acknowledge and restore to me

"*September 1st, 1845*"

I made no reply and she wrote again —

"*September 10th, 1845.*

' The last communication I made to you upon the subject of my position in your house, having remained unnoticed, I must now inform you that I have come to the determination not to submit any longer to be excluded from the care of my children, and being unable to obtain justice from you in this respect, will now leave this house whither I came solely for the purpose of discharging my duty, and being of use to my children All hope of any such result being at an end, in consequence of other influences to which they are subjected, and my remaining here being not only useless henceforward, but undoubtedly prejudicial to the children, I shall comply with my father's desire, and the advice of my friends and family, to return to England In doing so I am actuated by the same motives which brought me to this house, the desire of doing that which is best for my children. Should you at any future time, see fit to restore to me my proper position towards my children, be assured that NOTHING will prevent my resuming it, that God may yet incline your heart before it is too late to what is right in this respect, I pray most earnestly "

Mrs Butler was quite conscious that such precontrived epistles could produce no effect on me but, like her seemingly impulsive and resistless gushes in London, they might be shown, might be reserved for prospective emergencies, and might, to those who were unaware of the utter and puerile falsity of their contents, seem natural sequels to her correspondence with her "friends and family in England."

Of her own will had she abandoned her children for sixteen months, during which time their care and control *necessarily devolved upon myself.* When she came back I thought it prudent to continue, for a time at least, my supervision, until *I could ascertain what would probably be her future behaviour,* and judge as to the expediency and discretion of relinquishing them entirely to her. She was fully cognizant of my intention in this respect, and had acquiesced in it. In a letter to Mr Furness, I said, "She must bear in ' mind, however, that in consequence of her deser- "tion of the children I have been obliged for a year "past to assume the entire direction of them, and that "the arrangements I have made for their studies and "education, must in no way be interfered with."* Her written contract of agreement contained a similar provision,—"I will also conform to the arrangements "of his house, as I shall find them on entering it."† No restraint whatever was put upon the daily inter-course *between herself and children, it was entirely free;* but her deportment had not been such as to convince me of the *prudence of surrendering my charge.* My firm adherence to a sense of duty on this subject was the sole reason on which, to me, she ever pretended to justify or explain her final and abrupt departure. Her two letters, September 1st and 10th, assign no other motive or cause. As, how-

<hr/>

* See page 134.   † See page 147.

ever such a plea could avail as little in a court of
justice as in sound morals, she accommodated her
conscience to the necessities of her case, and charg-
ing me with "cruelty," exerted in her "*Narrative*"
all her remarkable powers of exaggeration, sophistry
and eloquence, to sustain this expedient afterthought
In her '*Answer*" to my petition for a divorce, she
says —" His conduct towards me for a long space of
   time before I so quitted and absented myself from
   his habitation, was designed and calculated, and such
' as to force me therefrom   I should have been jus-
"tified as I submit to the court even without such
"assent, license, approval, acquiescence, or design, in
"so quitting or absenting myself from the libellant's
"habitation by his cruel treatment of me and by such
"personal indignities offered to me by him, as ren-
"dered my condition intolerable and my life burthen-
"some "*   And again,—" His treatment of me was
"such, for a length of time, habitually, that I should
"have been warranted by the law of God and the
"land, to depart wholly from his house and never see
"him more, without incurring the charge of desertion
"or any other breach of my duty ' †

This imputation of "cruelty, ' and even of ' personal indignities," groundless and unsupported by
proof, but boldly and unblushingly made, was unknown
to me until the "*Narrative*" appeared   Her letters,
as I have remarked, warning me of her design, allege
nothing of the sort in the first, she observes,—" The
"removal of my children for a couple of months from
"the house into which I was admitted upon condi-
"tions which I embraced *solely* for the purpose of be-

* Mrs Butler's '*Narrative*' p 4   † Idem p 5

2 A

"ing with them, has of course cancelled those condi-
"tions I no longer feel myself in any way bound to
' observe them   *   *   *   *   This compact being,
"as far as I am concerned, at an end, I now write to
"you under the expectation that my children must
"soon return home, once more to entreat you to re-
"consider the arrangements in your house and family,
"and to reorganize them in a manner which shall
"place me in my right relations towards my children,
"and them in their proper relation to me   *   *   *
"I again appeal to you for your own sake, for that of
"the children, and for justice sake, to re-establish me
"in my rights and position as a mother" In the second, the very day before taking the long premedi-
tated and deliberate step, she wrote,—"I must now
"inform you that I have come to the determination
"not to submit any longer to be excluded from the
"care of my children, and being unable to obtain
"justice from you in this respect, will now leave this
"house   *   *   *   *   I shall comply with my fa-
· ther's desire, and the advice of my friends and fa-
"mily, to return to England In doing so, I am
"actuated by the same motives which brought me to
"this house, the desire of doing that which is best for
"my children" Not a word or syllable whispering
an intimation of "cruel treatment,' or " personal indignities ' The single point at issue, and that which
alone impels her movement, is explicitly declared to
be the care of the children, which she claimed as
hers, but which I thought it proper still to reserve as
mine This is undeniable and the subsequent resort
to other and novel pretences, such as "cruelty" and
" personal indignities," while it involves an admission

of the insufficiency of the only one on which she had
acted, did no more than give her the mere words of a
defence, and open a wide field for artificial sentiment
and disingenuous " *Narrative* "

The next day, September 11, 1845, she carried her
resolve into effect, leaving my house without my
consent, or even knowledge, and taking up her abode
at a public hotel She left the United States for
England in October following, and remained away
until the spring of 1848

During the period of eighteen months, which elapsed between her last desertion and her resumption of
her early professional occupation, she corresponded
freely with her children Her letters were mainly
descriptive of what she saw in Italy and other coun-
tries through which she travelled, and their letters to
her were dictated by their own minds and feelings I
interfered in no way, though naturally watchful of her
course After returning to public life, her letters became so objectionable as to compel me to place an
interdict upon further communications She wrote
what was not true, and what was designed and calculated to estrange and prejudice the minds and hearts
of my children from their father In mercy and justice to them and to myself 1 could not suffer this
They had no one to look to but me I was striving to
guide them aright, and my efforts would have been
worse than vain had their confidence been undermined
and destroyed

Her going again upon the stage totally extinguished
the hope, the faint and feeble hope, that she might at
some future day of more chastened and advanced age,
be enlightened by a just appreciation of her relations

and obligations   That act was the consummation of a sad career of error, which had engendered misery, strife and disunion at our hearth   Her prolonged misconduct had severed in succession every tie that united us. the fetters of the law alone remained and to remove those became thenceforward the object as well as the duty of my life

I have now done all that I proposed or wish to do in this printed pamphlet   One or two topics introduced into the "*Narrative*" of Mrs Butler as mere accessaries to her main drift, have intentionally been treated with contemptuous silence   They are mere efforts to insinuate injurious shades of disposition, taste or character, and these I prefer living down to formally contesting   My divorce leaves me with but a single object worth pursuing, the vindication of my conduct as a husband and a father from the elaborated tissue of accusations which, I presume, she placed upon record in the exulting expectation that it would thus be made, like a shirt of Nessus, to stick to me for ever   I cannot put this statement alongside of her "*Narrative*" that the law forbids   I can do better. I can deposit it in the hands of friends alike just and faithful, and I can mingle it with the testamentary memorials of paternal pride affection, and honour

PHILADELPHIA
OHN C CLARK, PRI
6S *Dock Street*

CPSIA information can be obtained at www.ICGtesting.com
Printed in the USA
BVOW11s1140140415

396068BV00012B/127/P